My JOULE SOUS VIDE COOKBOOK

101 DELICIOUS RECIPES WITH ILLUSTRATED INSTRUCTIONS FOR THE CHEFSTEPS JOULE IMMERSION CIRCULATOR

BY

JESSICA MICHEL

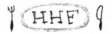

HHF PRESS
SAN FRANCISCO

MW00388847

Reader Reviews

"Wow, I really enjoyed the recipes in this book. My husband got excited when I made the baby back ribs, he said it was the best he'd ever had. I'm so in love with this gadget now, I'm planning to use it often!"

- Corinne G.

"Great primer on how to cook sous vide. My first steak turned out perfectly! The recipes are great—I've tried about a dozen of them so far. My favorites are the beef and lamb recipes, and surprisingly the flourless chocolate cake! "

- Sabrina M.

"Thanks! This book helped me get started after work, and I had an amazing meal at the end of the evening. Love the recipes!"

- Allison G.

"Today a succulent beef brisket cooked itself at home while I was at work. Are you kidding me? This is too easy... I've recommended it to all of my friends."

- Lewis C.

"At last I know the secret to getting extremely tender and flavorful steaks. This even works for burgers and fried chicken. I'm pretty sold on the joule and these recipes are wonderful."

- Mary T.

Legal Notice

The information contained in this book is for entertainment purposes only. The content represents the opinion of the author and is based on the author's personal experience and observations. The author does not assume any liability whatsoever for the use of or inability to use any or all information contained in this book, and accepts no responsibility for any loss or damages of any kind that may be incurred by the reader as a result of actions arising from the use of information in this book. Use this information at your own risk.

The author reserves the right to make any changes he or she deems necessary to future versions of the publication to ensure its accuracy.

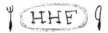

COPYRIGHT © 2017 Healthy Happy Foodie Press.

All rights reserved.

ISBN-13:978-1976595042
ISBN-10:1976595045

Published in the United States of America by Healthy Happy Foodie Press.

www.HHFpress.com

Table Of Contents

1

Why You Need This Book

Congratulations on your purchase of the Joule sous vide system While there are many sous vide immersion circulators on the market these days, the Joule sous vide system by Chef Steps is superior in every way. As you are about to find out, your Joule is capable of amazing versatility and offers features that are unparalleled in other sous vide units. In short, you have purchased the most advanced, easy to use, and powerful sous vide unit on the market. This guide will provide you with everything you need in order to become an expert sous vide chef in no time with the Joule sous vide system.

In addition to a comprehensive guide to the science and history of sous vide cooking, we will also go into depth about how to get the absolute most out of your Joule every time you use it. You will soon realize that you can cook nearly anything with your Joule, and best of all, you will easily be able to cook everything to perfection. Once you start using your Joule, you will wonder how you ever cooked without it. Now let's get started by discussing the remarkable and revolutionary features of the Joule.

The Remarkable Features of The Joule

Innovative Design

The first thing you might notice about the Joule when you take it out of the box is how simple its design is. While the simplicity of the design is certainly attractive, there is another reason for the Joule's simple appearance: The Joule is designed to be used in professional cooking settings, everyday. This means that it needs to be durable enough to handle fast paced restaurant environments even though it is intended mostly for home use. The body is made from extruded polycarbonate for maximum strength, and the top and bottom are constructed from high-grade stainless steel to ensure that your Joule lasts for years to come.

If you have spent any time comparing the Joule to other sous vide units, you may notice something quite different about the

Joule's appearance: It has no digital display. While this may seem strange at first, it actually makes the Joule an even more durable and convenient piece of equipment. First of all, displays are prone to breaking. They contain many fragile parts that can become damaged through prolonged use. The Joule remedies this by eliminating the display from the unit itself, and instead allows you to control all of the Joule's functions by utilizing a revolutionary smartphone app. The other downside to having an on-board display is that a display adds unnecessary weight to the unit making it bulkier and heavier. The designers of the Joule decided to eliminate the display and, in the process, made the Joule so small and light that you can take it with you wherever you go.

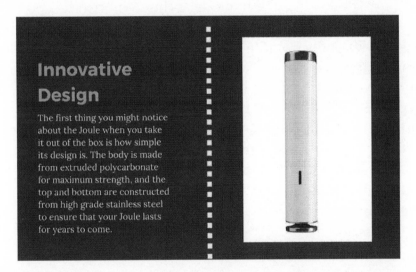

Innovative Design

The first thing you might notice about the Joule when you take it out of the box is how simple its design is. The body is made from extruded polycarbonate for maximum strength, and the top and bottom are constructed from high grade stainless steel to ensure that your Joule lasts for years to come.

The only button on the Joule is the On and Off button, making the Joule the simplest sous vide unit to use. While there is no on-board display, there are three LED lights that let you know the status of the Joule at any given time. A yellow light means that the Joule is in the process of heating water, a green light means the water has reached its target temperature, and a red light means that something has gone wrong. Usually a red light will indicate that there is not enough water in the cooking vessel. These status indicators can also be monitored via the Joule's smartphone app.

On / Off Button

Because of the simplicity of its construction, the Joule couldn't be easier to clean. Simply remove the foot piece and wipe with a wet cloth or sponge. That's it. To clean the rest of the unit, just wipe it with a wet cloth. The Joule is completely sealed so you will never have to worry about dirt getting inside the unit. Because the Joule is so compact, you can store it almost anywhere. And since it is constructed using only the most durable materials you don't have to worry about keeping it in a bulky case in order to keep it safe. This means that you can take it with you on the go and cook perfect sous vide meals anywhere.

High Power

Truly, one of the most remarkable features of the Joule is its power. By using the power of a thick-film heater, the Joule efficiently produces heat faster than any other sous vide unit on the market. This means that you don't have to waste time waiting for your water bath to heat up. And because the Joule is so powerful, you can heat up to twenty liters of water in no time. But you don't have to use a large water bath if you don't want to. Unlike many sous vide units, the Joule can cook in water as shallow as one and a half inches. This is thanks to the way the bottom of the Joule is designed. In any sous vide unit, the water is drawn into the unit through vents in the bottom, heated, and then circulated back into the water bath by the internal motor. Most sous vide units are constructed in a way that requires at least four to five inches of water. The Joule, on the other hand, has a fluted foot that makes direct contact with the bottom of the water bath so it doesn't require nearly as much water.

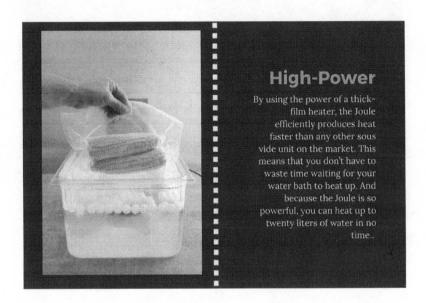

High-Power

By using the power of a thick-film heater, the Joule efficiently produces heat faster than any other sous vide unit on the market. This means that you don't have to waste time waiting for your water bath to heat up. And because the Joule is so powerful, you can heat up to twenty liters of water in no time..

Extremely Versatile

The bottom of the Joule is also designed for another unique purpose: versatility. Most sous vide units require a certain type of vessel in order to function properly. The Cambro is the most common sous vide vessel. It is a rather large clear plastic basin that can be difficult to store, and often requires using more water than necessary. Thanks to the fluted foot design of the Joule you can cook in virtually any vessel, from the standard Cambro, to a simple bowl, the kitchen sink, or even a coffee mug. The magnetic foot secures the Joule to any stainless-steel surface or the optional clip will secure the Joule to any aluminum or non-metallic vessel. This type of versatile design and construction alone makes the Joule more advanced and powerful than any other sous vide unit, but what really sets the Joule apart is its amazing bluetooth smartphone interface.

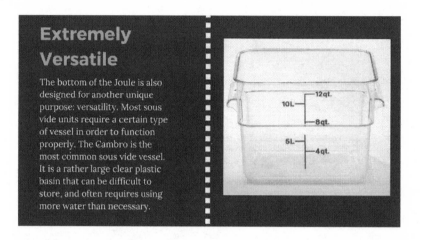

Extremely Versatile

The bottom of the Joule is also designed for another unique purpose: versatility. Most sous vide units require a certain type of vessel in order to function properly. The Cambro is the most common sous vide vessel. It is a rather large clear plastic basin that can be difficult to store, and often requires using more water than necessary.

As we mentioned before, the Joule has no on-board interface. To utilize all of the Joule's features you will download a smartphone app that works with both the iPhone and Android platforms. Everything you will need to control every aspect of the Joule is contained in this app, and because the app is constantly being updated and improved, you will always have access to the most advanced features available. The app itself is easy to use and intuitive so that you will be able to start cooking immediately. We will discuss everything you need to know about the app in order to install it and get cooking as quickly as possible. Now let's spend a moment discussing how sous vide cooking works.

2

Understanding Sous Vide

What is Sous Vide?

Quite simply, sous vide cooking is a method in which food is sealed in a bag, submerged in a water bath, and gradually brought to a specific temperature in order to ensure perfectly reliable results. There are many advantages to sous vide cooking, but the most obvious is that it is virtually impossible to overcook your food. Since modern sous vide cooking relies on specialized equipment like the Joule, maintaining a constant water temperature is effortless. The Joule makes sure the water is always set to the exact temperature that you desire, the food in the water bath will never rise above or fall below that temperature, so you never run the risk of over or undercooking anything.

Perfect cooking temperatures, however, aren't the only benefit of sous vide cooking. Because your food is encased in a sealed bag while it cooks, you can also add seasonings or marinades to the bag, and these flavors will be locked into your food as it cooks. One of the reasons many restaurant chefs rely on sous vide cooking is because sous vide can achieve more robust and flavorful foods without any extra effort. As sous vide becomes more and more popular, professional chefs and home cooks alike are finding more interesting uses for this method of cooking. This book will teach you how to get the most out of your sous vide cooking adventures using your Joule cooking system. From vegetables to meats to dessert, we will give you all the tips and techniques necessary to become a sous vide master chef in no time.

Sous Vide Tools

The great thing about cooking sous vide with the Joule is that you don't need a lot of complicated cooking equipment. The Joule is the most versatile sous vide unit on the market partly because it allows you to cook in almost any container. Typically, you would use a plexiglass Cambro vessel to cook sous vide, but the Joule allows you to cook in a large bowl, the kitchen sink, or anything that holds enough water to fully submerge the food you would like to cook.

Other than maintaining a constant temperature, the other important feature of sous vide cooking is the "vide" or vacuum. In order for your food to cook evenly, it needs to have even contact with the water bath. For this reason, you will need to use a method for sealing the food in a plastic bag. Simple food sealing devices like the FoodSaver® or Seal-a-Meal® make the process fast, easy, and reliable. But if you don't feel like purchasing another piece of equipment, you can achieve a good seal using the water displacement method. Simply place your food in a zipper lock bag and seal all but a small corner of the zipper lock. Then, slowly submerge the bag in the water bath (make sure the water isn't too hot when you do this). As you submerge the bag, the air will be forced out through the unsealed corner of the bag. When only this corner is above the surface of the water, pinch the zipper lock shut and all of the air will be removed.

NOTE: When choosing zipper lock bags, make sure to check the packaging to make sure the bags are BPA free. Because the dangers of BPA are now well known, most bags are already certified BPA free and are safe to use for sous vide cooking.

A History of Sous Vide Cooking

The name—sous vide—is French for "under vacuum" which describes the main feature of sous vide cooking. In order to successfully cook sous vide it is necessary to submerge the food in a water bath in a vacuum-sealed bag. Sous vide is a cooking method that originated in France as early as 1799 as a method for reliable cooking and food preservation. Without special equipment, however, maintaining a constant temperature was a challenge and required constant supervision. Cooks of this era also didn't have the luxury of modern plastic bags and relied instead on animal intestines and bladders (which were not very reliable for maintaining a perfect air tight seal!). Because of this the method didn't become popular at first. It wasn't until the 1970s, when sous vide immersion circulators became available, that French chefs discovered that sous vide was the perfect way to cook fois gras.

They found that using this method, they were able to cook the delicate goose liver pate and maintain its original appearance, and it also helped to retain the rich fat while cooking thoroughly. It wasn't long before other chefs began seeing the benefits of sous vide cooking. Now it is a widely used method for cooking many different types of foods and is found in professional kitchens around the world.

Who Uses Sous Vide?

While sous vide cooking was originally intended for high-end professional kitchens, home cooks are embracing the method for a variety of reasons. For beginner chefs, it is the perfect way to ensure that you never over or undercook food. Busy professionals will appreciate the fact that you can sous vide while at work all day and come home to a perfectly cooked meal that requires only minutes to finish. Even children can learn to cook sous vide because there is no direct heat source. That means no burns and no accidental fires to worry about. And considering how easy and fun the Joule is to use, there's no excuse not to sous vide.

Nutritional Benefits of Sous Vide Cooking

Lock in the nutrients! Everyone is concerned about getting proper nutrition, but what you may not know is that certain cooking methods can actually destroy some of the vital nutrients that our bodies need. Many types of food, including meats and vegetables can lose a great deal of their nutrients while being cooked over high heat. Some fat based nutrients can simply break down and become less beneficial, while others are lost as the juices cook out of the food. With sous vide cooking, however, you don't have to worry about losing those precious nutrients. Because sous vide uses much lower temperatures, the nutrients remain intact. And since the juices are all contained within the vacuum-sealed bag, they don't have anywhere to go.

Using traditional cooking methods, it's nearly impossible to cook without the use of fat. And while certain oils, such as olive oil, do have health benefits, others, like butter, are just adding unnecessary fat to your diet. Since food cooked with the sous vide method doesn't touch a hot surface, no oil is required in the cooking process. And since studies have shown that oils heated to high temperature can cause a variety of health issues, sous vide cooking completely eliminates this concern.

You may have heard that sous vide is a great way to get perfect results for meat, but sous vide is also a perfect way to get the best flavor from fruits and vegetables. Unlike steaming, sous vide actually concentrates the flavor of vegetables for a richer, tastier dish that everyone will love. You can also make robust fruit compotes and sauces without adding sugar. Simply set your Joule for a long cook time and allow fruits to break down into a delicious sauce on their own, using their own natural sugars.

If you're looking for a great way to add protein to your diet while avoiding fat, sous vide is a great way to make lean meats tender and juicy. Much like how professional barbecue chefs cook tougher cuts low and slow for fall off the bone texture, you can get the same results with your Joule simply by allowing those lean cuts to cook for long periods of time. And since sous vide cooking doesn't require any supervision, you can leave it on overnight while you sleep or while you're out of the house.

3

How to Use Your Joule

Sous vide cooking can seem challenging, but the Joule makes it as easy as pressing a couple of buttons. When you unbox your Joule, you will notice how simple it is. The unit plugs into any outlet and is ready to cook immediately.

- The first thing you will want to do is download the smartphone app, which will allow you to control the Joule from anywhere as long as you have a WiFi or Bluetooth connection. The app is available for both Android and iPhone. Once you have installed the app, it's time to cook.

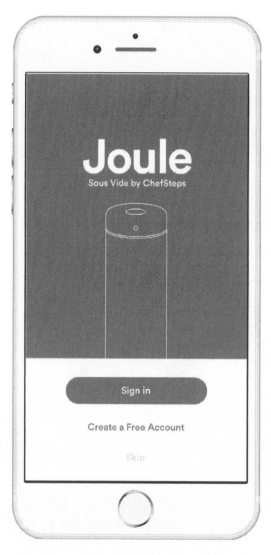

- Unlike other sous vide units, the Joule can cook in nearly any vessel. If you choose to cook in a stainless-steel pot, the Joule's magnetic foot will automatically latch onto the bottom and will keep the unit perfectly upright.

- For aluminum, plastic, or ceramic vessels, you can attach the Joule to the side by using the built-in clip. Simply slide the clip over the edge of the vessel and you're ready to go. The clip is designed to firmly attach the Joule to any vessel.

- Once you have your Joule attached to a vessel that is filled with water, you will sync the Joule to the app. Simply open the app and go to Settings.

- From there, click on device settings and the app will recognize your Joule. If you are within Bluetooth range it will give you the option of connecting via Bluetooth or WiFi.

- If you are out of Bluetooth range (about thirty feet) you will only have the ability to connect via WiFi. When you choose the connection option that you prefer, the app will activate your Joule using your home WiFi network. Once you're connected, the Joule will start by asking you what you want to cook.

- More seasoned sous vide chefs can go straight to the menu and select the temperature and time settings. These settings will allow you to set a precise temperature for the water bath as well as a cooking time.

- For beginners, the app has a setting for almost every type of food you can think of already programmed into it, and it will walk you through how to cook nearly anything. Just follow the prompts on the app.

1 SYNC THE JOULE

Open the Joule App and go to Settings. Click it and the App will recognize your Joule.

2 CONNECT

If you are within a Bluetooth range, it will give you the option of connecting via Bluetooth or WIFI.

3 CHOOSE YOUR RECIPE

Once you're connected, the Joule will start asking you of what you want to cook.

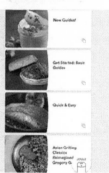

- Simply select the type of food you want to cook (a steak) and how you would like it cooked (medium rare) and the Joule will set the temperature and a timer.

- When your food is finished, the Joule will send a notification to your phone letting you know that your food has finished cooking. You can even start and stop the Joule from anywhere, using the app.

4 TIME & TEMP

Select how you would like your food is cooked (medium rare) and the Joule will set the temperature and a timer.

5 DESCRIBE MORE

Describe your food a little more by choosing the thickness of your food and if it is fresh or frozen. Then, click the "start" button.

6 DONE

When your food is finished, the Joule will send a notification to your phone letting you know that your food has finished cooking.

- The Joule also has a revolutionary feature called "Visual Doneness" that takes even more guesswork out of the cooking process.

- If you're not sure what temperature you want to achieve, simply choose the type of food you want to cook and scroll through the list of pictures of that food at various stages of doneness.

- Then select the picture that looks right to you and the Joule will automatically cook to that temperature. It really is that easy!

- When you're finished cooking and need to clean and store the Joule simply remove it from the water bath, wipe all over with a damp cloth and store in a dry place.

- The Joule is designed to repel dirt and food particles so there is no need to scrub it or use any type of cleaning solution. From start to finish, the Joule is the most efficient, easiest to use sous vide unit on the market.

4

Pro Tips

Get Even More Flavor Using Seasonings

We've already discussed how and why sous vide is such a great method for making perfectly cooked food, but if you really want to get the most out of the experience, seasoning in the bag is the way to go. If you pre-season your food, the vacuum seal will press those delicious flavors right into the food and keep them there for the entire cooking time. Never worry about reapplying seasoning or basting again. By cooking sous vide, you can be assured that your seasonings will stick and remain evenly distributed without any work. To enhance the flavor of things like chicken breast even more, you can add a couple of tablespoons of olive oil to the bag to create the most tender chicken you've ever had. If you're using your sous vide to make barbecued meats, a couple of drops of liquid smoke in the bag will simulate that distinctive wood smoke flavor very well.

A Great Sear Is Another Way to Add Flavor

You've used your Joule to cook your food to the desired temperature, but what's next? Well, certain foods like vegetables and fish are often ready to eat right out of the bag. But things like beef or chicken can benefit from one more step. If you're making a nice New York Strip steak, your Joule has cooked the inside to whatever temperature you prefer, but most of us like a nice dark sear on a steak. Once you're happy with the internal temperature, heat a pan (preferably a cast iron pan) to the point of smoking and add a tablespoon of vegetable oil. Drop your steak in the pan for just a couple of minutes on each side to achieve a nice dark sear. To enhance the sear further, try putting a tablespoon of butter in the pan while searing for an even darker, crisper crust. The high heat will sear the outside nicely, but the inside will stay juicy and rare.

With Sous Vide There's No Need to Rest Meat

Generally, when cooking things like beef, you will need to rest it after cooking. Depending on how large a piece of meat you have, this time could range anywhere from ten minutes for an average steak, to about an hour for a rib roast. The reason meat needs to rest is to give the cooler internal temperature of the meat time to even out with the hotter external temperature of the surface of the meat. Allowing the meat to rest ensures that the juices within the meat will be fully absorbed and not lost when the meat is cut. When meat is cooked sous vide, this difference between the internal and external temperatures does not exist, which means meat cooked sous vide can be served right out of the bag. Or right out of the pan if you're searing it.

Cook Low and Slow for Fall-Off-The-Bone Meats

Earlier, we mentioned the fact that cooking sous vide is a great way to make your favorite barbecue dishes in your kitchen without the hassle of using a smoker, but how does this really work? Meats like pork shoulder and brisket are delicious, but in order to get that fall off the bone texture they have to be cooked for a long time. This means that you either have to smoke them at low temperatures or keep them in the oven all day. This can be tricky if you have a busy schedule. But with sous vide cooking you can safely cook food all day without supervision. If you want to make perfect fall of the bone meats at home, season the outside of the meat with your favorite rub, seal it, and adjust your Joule to 165 degrees. Then submerge the meat in the water and cook for twelve hours.

Never Cook Too Low for Too Long

Sous vide cooking is one of the easiest and safest ways to cook almost anything, but if food is cooked at too low a temperature for too long, you run the risk of food borne illness. Foods like fish are best at around 120-125 degrees, but they only require around a half an hour in the sous vide to cook properly. After more than three hours at such a low temperature, bacteria can begin to multiply and become a health risk. A good rule of thumb is: Foods that are best at a low temperature like fish should only cook for a short time (less than three hours), and foods that need a long cook time need to be cooked at high temperatures (165 degrees and up). If you stick to these basic guidelines your food will always be 100% safe to eat.

5

Breakfast

Perfect Poached Eggs

Servings: 2 | Prep Time: 2 minutes | Cook Time: 45 minutes

Your Joule holds water at such a precise temperature that it takes all of the guesswork out of poached eggs cooked exactly how you prefer them.

Ingredients:

2 large eggs

Instructions:

1. Fill a water bath and set your Joule to 145F/62C.

2. Submerge the eggs and cook for 45 minutes. When eggs are nearly cooked, heat a small pot of water to boiling.

3. Remove the eggs from the water bath, and gently remove the shells. Place the eggs in the boiling water for 10 seconds and carefully remove them. For a slightly firmer yolk, boil an additional 15 seconds.

Nutritional Info: Calories: 72, Sodium: 70 mg, Dietary Fiber: 0 g, Fat: 5 g, Carbs: 7.4 g, Protein: 6.3 g.

Ham and Egg Scramble

Servings: 4 | Prep time: 10 minutes | Cook time: 40 minutes

This hearty scramble is a great way to start the day and is sure to impress the whole family. Your Joule ensures that your eggs will be cooked perfectly with a rich natural flavor.

Ingredients:

8 large eggs

1/4-pound Black Forest ham

1/2 cup sharp cheddar cheese, grated

2 tablespoons butter, melted

1/2 teaspoon salt

1/2 cup whole milk

Instructions:

1. Fill a water bath and set your Joule to 170F/76C.

2. In a medium bowl, scramble the eggs and add the ham, cheese, butter, salt, and milk. Mix well and pour into a zipper lock bag. Remove all air from the bag and place in the water bath for 20 minutes.

3. Remove the bag from the water bath and, using your hands, mix the contents. Then place back in the water bath for an additional 20 minutes. Remove the bag from the water bath and serve immediately.

Nutritional Info: Calories: 315, Sodium: 941 mg, Dietary Fiber: 0.4 g, Fat: 23.8 g, Carbs: 3.4 g, Protein: 21.9 g.

Sous Vide French Toast

Servings: 4 | Prep time: 10 minutes | Cook time: 60 minutes

This classic favorite has many variations, but for delicate, custardy results try using your Joule for spectacular French toast every time.

Ingredients:

8 large eggs

3/4 cups milk

1 teaspoon vanilla extract

1/2 teaspoon salt

4 thick slices of bread

2 tablespoons butter

Instructions:

1. Fill a water bath and set your Joule to 147F/67C.

2. In a large bowl, combine the eggs, milk, vanilla, and salt, and mix well. Soak the bread in the egg mixture and place in a zipper lock bag. Remove all the air from the bag and submerge in the water bath for 60 minutes.

3. When you're almost finished cooking, heat a skillet with the butter over medium heat. Remove the bread from the water bath and place in the skillet until lightly browned on each side. Serve immediately with maple syrup or powdered sugar.

Nutritional Info: Calories: 244, Sodium: 555 mg, Dietary Fiber: 0.2 g, Fat: 16.9 g, Carbs: 7.7 g, Protein: 14.8 g.

Classic Eggs Benedict

Servings: 4 | Prep time: 30 minutes | Cook time: 30 minutes

This breakfast classic is usually reserved for restaurants, but your Joule makes it so easy that you can make it at home anytime you want.

Ingredients:

4 eggs, poached

4 slices Black Forest or tavern ham

4 English muffins, toasted

For the sauce:

1 cup white wine

3 tablespoons champagne or white wine vinegar

1 teaspoon fresh thyme

6 egg yolks

1 cup unsalted butter, melted

1 tablespoon lemon juice

Instructions:

1. Fill a water bath and set your Joule to 145F/62C.
2. In a medium saucepan heat the wine, vinegar, and thyme until boiling and simmer for 10 minutes. Remove from heat and pour into a blender with the egg yolks and puree until smooth.
3. Pour the mixture into a large zipper lock bag and submerge in the water bath for 30 minutes.
4. While the Hollandaise sauce cooks, poach the eggs and toast the muffins. Remove the Hollandaise sauce from the water bath and stir. You can also keep the sauce in the water bath for up to 2 hours if you're not ready to serve right away.

5. To assemble, Place the muffins on plates, top with ham, a poached egg, and cover with Hollandaise sauce. Garnish with chopped chives and serve immediately.

Nutritional Info: Calories: 752, Sodium: 740 mg, Dietary Fiber: 2.1 g, Fat: 58.7 g, Carbs: 28.9 g, Protein: 15.7 g.

Red Pepper Frittata

Servings: 3 | Prep time: 30 minutes | Cook time: 60 minutes

This fun take on a classic egg scramble is sweet and savory, and thanks to your Joule, it will be cooked perfectly tender every time.

Ingredients:

6 large eggs

1 red bell pepper, diced

1 teaspoon salt

1 tablespoon butter

3 tablespoons yellow onion, finely chopped

1/4 cup milk

1/2 teaspoon red pepper flakes

Instructions:

1. Fill a water bath and set your Joule to 176F/80C.

2. In a medium skillet over medium heat, melt the butter and add the bell pepper, onion, and pepper flakes. Cook until the onions and peppers are tender. Remove from heat.

3. In a large bowl, scramble the eggs and add the salt, onion and pepper mixture, and milk. Stir well and pour into 3 mason jars. Secure the lids and submerge in the water bath for 60 minutes.

4. Remove the jars from the water bath and allow to cool slightly before servings.

Nutritional Info: Calories: 205, Sodium: 953 mg, Dietary Fiber: 0.8 g, Fat: 14.4 g, Carbs: 5.9 g, Protein: 13.8 g.

Canadian Bacon

Servings: 8 | Prep time: 5 minutes | Cook time: 6 to 12 hours

This savory breakfast treat is made perfectly tender and juicy with some help from your Joule sous vide system. The secret is cooking low and slow for amazing texture.

Ingredients:

8 thick slices tavern ham

1 teaspoon vegetable oil

Instructions:

1. Fill a water bath and set your Joule to 145F/62C.
2. Place the ham slices side by side in a large zipper lock bag and remove all of the air from the bag.
3. Submerge the bag in the water bath for at least 6 and up to 12 hours.
4. Heat a large skillet with the oil and remove the ham from the water bath. Place each slice of ham onto the skillet and cook, pressing down on the ham with a spatula until lightly browned.
5. Serve immediately.

Nutritional Info: Calories: 24, Sodium: 93 mg, Dietary Fiber: 0 g, Fat: 0.6 g, Carbs: 0.3 g, Protein: 3 g.

Bacon and Asparagus Egg White Omelet

Servings: 2 | Prep time: 10 minutes | Cook time: 40 minutes

This healthy omelet is the perfect way to start the day, with a combination of nutrient rich vegetables and protein packed egg whites.

Ingredients:

4 egg whites

4 slices bacon, cut into small pieces

1/4-pound asparagus, chopped into small pieces

1 tablespoon vegetable oil

1 teaspoon salt

Instructions:

1. Fill a water bath and set your Joule to 170F/76C.

2. In a large bowl, whip the egg whites and add the salt.

3. In a medium saucepan over medium heat, add the oil and asparagus and cook for 5 minutes. Add the bacon and cook until the bacon is crispy. Remove from heat.

4. Add the bacon and asparagus mixture to the egg whites and divide into two zipper lock bags. Remove all air from the bags and submerge in the water bath for 20 minutes. Remove the bags from the water, turnover and continue cooking for an additional 20 minutes. Remove the bags from the water and serve immediately.

Nutritional Info: Calories: 117, Sodium: 277 mg, Dietary Fiber: 1.2 g, Fat: 7.8 g, Carbs: 2.7 g, Protein: 9.2 g.

Sous Vide Yogurt

Servings: 10| Prep time: 5 minutes | Cook time: 4 hours

Yogurt is packed with protein, nutrients, and great flavor. For perfect yogurt made at home, your Joule will provide perfect results for creamy, delicious yogurt any time you want.

Ingredients:

1/2-gallon whole milk

2 tablespoons Greek yogurt

Instructions:

1. Fill a water bath and set your Joule to 180F/82C.

2. Pour the milk into a large zipper lock bag. Stir well and remove all air from the bag. Submerge the bag in the water bath for 10 minutes.

3. Reset the temperature on your Joule to 110F/43C. You can add ice to the water to make it cool down faster. Then, reset the temperature to 115F/46C and add the yogurt to the milk, stir well, and reseal the bag. Submerge it in the water bath and cook for 3 hours.

4. Remove the bag from the water bath, allow to cool, and use a mesh strainer to strain out the whey. If you find that the yogurt is too thick after straining, you can stir in some of the whey.

Nutritional Info: Calories: 145, Sodium: 90 mg, Dietary Fiber:0 g, Fat: 7.1 g, Carbs: 10.3 g, Protein: 10.2 g.

6

Vegetables

Creamed Baby Peas

Servings: 8 | Prep time: 5 minutes | Cook time: 60 minutes

This simple dish is packed with robust flavors and sweet notes for a perfectly balanced side dish that can accompany practically anything.

Ingredients:

1 pound baby peas

3/4 cups heavy cream

1 shallot, finely minced

1/2 teaspoon salt

1/4 teaspoon black pepper

2 teaspoons vegetable oil

Instructions:

1. Fill a water bath and set your Joule to 185F/85C.

2. While the water bath is heating, heat the oil in a medium saucepan over medium heat. Add the shallots and cook until tender and fragrant. Remove from heat and allow to cool.

3. In a large zipper lock bag, combine the peas, shallots, cream, salt, and pepper. Remove all air from the bag and submerge in the water bath for 60 minutes. Remove from the bath and serve immediately. If you're not quite ready to serve, the bag can remain in the water bath for another 30 minutes.

Nutritional Info: Calories: 76, Sodium: 315 mg, Dietary Fiber: 1.8 g, Fat: 5.3 g, Carbs: 4.9 g, Protein: 1.6 g.

Sous Vide Spicy Green Beans

Servings: 4 | Prep time: 10 minutes | Cook time 60 minutes

A perfect way to cook tender green beans and add a delightful kick of heat that will be sure to leave your guests asking for more.

Ingredients:

1 pound fresh green beans

1 tablespoon butter

1 teaspoon red pepper flakes

1/2 teaspoon garlic powder

1/2 teaspoon onion powder

Instructions:

1. Fill a water bath and set your Joule to 185F/85C.
2. In a large zipper lock bag, combine the green beans, butter, pepper flakes, garlic, and onion and mix well. Remove all air from the bag and submerge in the water bath for 60 minutes.
3. Remove bag from the water bath and stir again before serving.

Nutritional Info: Calories: 64, Sodium: 28 mg, Dietary Fiber: 4 g, Fat: 3.1 g, Carbs: 8.8 g, Protein: 2.2 g.

Balsamic Onions

Servings: 10 | Prep time: 10 minutes | Cook time: 3 hours

These sweet onions are perfect as a garnish or topping for burgers or pizza. In fact, they're so flavorful you may find yourself pairing them with steaks and salads.

Ingredients:

2 yellow onions

2 tablespoons olive oil

1 tablespoon balsamic vinegar

1 tablespoon sugar

1/4 teaspoon salt

1/4 teaspoon black pepper

Instructions:

1. Fill a water bath and set your Joule to 185F/85C.
2. Slice the onions into thin strips and combine with the oil, vinegar, sugar, salt, and pepper in a large zipper lock bag. Remove all air from the bag and submerge in the water bath for 3 hours.
3. Remove the bag from the water bath, stir the contents well and refrigerate until cool before using.

Nutritional Info: Calories: 38, Sodium: 59 mg, Dietary Fiber: 0.5 g, Fat: 2.8 g, Carbs: 3.3 g, Protein: 0.3 g.

Asparagus with Lardons

Servings: 4 | Prep time: 10 minutes | Cook time: 60 minutes

This savory vegetable treat goes will with meat or fish dishes. To add a kick of heat, try adding a pinch of Cayenne pepper to the mix.

Ingredients:

1 pound asparagus

1/4-pound bacon, cut into small strips

1 tablespoon olive oil

1/4 teaspoon black pepper

Instructions:

1. Fill a water bath and set your Joule to 185F/85C.
2. While the water bath is heating, bring a medium saucepan to medium heat and cook the bacon until slightly crisp. Remove the bacon from the pan and rest on paper towels.
3. In a large zipper lock bag, combine the asparagus, bacon, oil, and pepper and mix well. Remove all air from the bag and submerge in the water bath for 60 minutes. Remove the bag from the water bath and serve immediately.

Nutritional Info: Calories: 206, Sodium: 657 mg, Dietary Fiber: 2.4 g, Fat: 15.5 g, Carbs: 4.9 g, Protein: 13 g.

Perfect Corn on the Cob

Servings: 4 | Prep time: 5 minutes | Cook time: 40 minutes

This picnic favorite can be cooked a number of ways, but using your Joule will guarantee perfectly flavorful and succulent corn any time.

Ingredients:

4 ears of corn, shucked

4 tablespoons butter

1/4 tablespoon black pepper

Instructions:

1. Fill a water bath and set your Joule to 180F/82C.

2. In a large zipper lock bag, add the corn, butter and pepper. Remove all air from the bag and submerge in the water bath for 20 minutes.

3. Remove the bag from the water bath and agitate to make sure the butter is coating the corn evenly. Place the bag back in the water bath and cook an additional 20 minutes. Remove the bag from the water bath and enjoy.

Nutritional Info: Calories: 235, Sodium: 105 mg, Dietary Fiber: 4.3 g, Fat: 13.3 g, Carbs: 29.3 g, Protein: 5.2 g.

Miso Glazed Eggplant

Servings: 4 | Prep time: 20 minutes | Cook time: 3 hours

This richly flavored eggplant dish has hints of sweet and savory with a texture that pairs well with both meat and fish dishes. Or it can be a savory vegetarian entree on its own.

Ingredients:

1 eggplant, sliced into rounds, 1/2-inch-thick

1/4 cup white miso paste

2 tablespoons soy sauce

2 tablespoons sake

1 teaspoon sesame oil

1 tablespoon sugar

Green onion, for serving

Instructions:

1. Fill a water bath and set your Joule to 185F/85C.

2. Place eggplant into zipper lock bags. Remove all air from the bags and submerge in the water bath for 2 1/2 hours.

3. When the eggplant is almost finished, heat a medium saucepan over low heat and add the miso paste, sake, soy sauce, sesame oil and sugar. Heat until combined and smooth. Remove from heat.

4. Remove the eggplant from the water bath and lay the rounds on a baking sheet. Dry the rounds with paper towels and brush on a coating of the miso glaze. Set your broiler to high and broil the eggplant until they begin to caramelize. Remove from the broiler and garnish with the green onions.

Nutritional Info: Calories: 62, Sodium: 451 mg, Dietary Fiber: 0.1 g, Fat: 1.1 g, Carbs: 3.7 g, Protein: 0.5 g.

Springtime Ratatouille

Servings: 6 | Prep time: 30 minutes | Cook time: 2 hours

This delightful fresh vegetable dish melds flavors for a perfect balance of earthy and sweet for a ratatouille that you will want to make any time of year.

Ingredients:

3 zucchinis, cut into small pieces

3 Roma tomatoes, cut into small pieces

2 red bell peppers, cut into small pieces

1 eggplant, cut into small pieces

1 yellow onion, diced

5 cloves garlic, roughly chopped

1 teaspoon salt

4 tablespoons olive oil

Instructions:

1. Fill a water bath and set your Joule to 185F/85C.
2. Place the tomatoes into a large zipper lock bag and add 1 tablespoon of olive oil and one clove of garlic. Remove all the air from the bag. In another zipper lock bag, place the remaining vegetables, garlic, salt, and olive oil. Place both bags in the water bath and cook for 1 1/2 hours.
3. After 30 minutes, remove the bag with the tomatoes and set aside.
4. Allow the other bag to cook an additional 90 minutes.
5. Discard the garlic and mix the tomatoes with the rest of the vegetables in a large bowl.

Nutritional Info: Calories: 150, Sodium: 404 mg, Dietary Fiber: 5.5 g, Fat: 9.9 g, Carbs: 15.7 g, Protein: 3.2 g.

Savory Cauliflower Mash

Servings: 4 | Prep time: 20 minutes | Cook time: 45 minutes

This mash makes an excellent stand in for mashed potatoes if you're looking for a delicious way to eat more vegetables and still have a rich, comforting side dish.

Ingredients:

1 large cauliflower, roughly chopped

1 cup chicken broth

4 tablespoons butter

Salt and pepper to taste

Instructions:

1. Fill a water bath, and set your Joule to 185F/85C.

2. Place the cauliflower, broth, and butter in a large zipper lock bag. Remove all air in the bag and submerge in the water bath for 45 minutes.

3. Remove the bag from the water, strain the cauliflower and place in a blender. Blend until smooth adding salt and pepper to taste. Serve immediately.

Nutritional Info: Calories: 147, Sodium: 316 mg, Dietary Fiber: 3.6 g, Fat: 12 g, Carbs: 7.9 g, Protein: 4.2 g.

Sweet Glazed Carrots

Servings: 6 | Prep time: 10 minutes | Cook time: 45 minutes

This dish pairs well with almost anything because of a perfect balance between sweet and savory flavors.

Ingredients:

1 pound baby carrots, peeled

2 tablespoons butter

2 tablespoons maple syrup

1 teaspoon salt

1/4 teaspoon pepper

Instructions:

1. Fill a water bath and set your Joule to 180F/82C.

2. Combine all ingredients in a large zipper lock bag. Remove all the air from the bag and submerge in the water bath for 45 minutes.

3. When the carrots are nearly finished in the water bath, set your broiler to high. Remove the carrots from the water bath and arrange on a baking sheet. Broil for 3 to 5 minutes or until the glaze caramelized slightly. Serve immediately.

Nutritional Info: Calories: 78, Sodium: 474 mg, Dietary Fiber: 2.2 g, Fat: 4 g, Carbs: 10.8 g, Protein: 0.5 g.

Sous Vide Country Potato Salad

Servings: 4 | Prep time: 20 minutes | Cook time: 30 minutes

This potato salad is perfect for backyard barbecues or any summer meal. Your Joule makes sure everything is cooked to an absolutely perfect texture.

Ingredients:

2 cups red potatoes, cut into large chunks

1 tablespoon yellow mustard

1 tablespoon sour cream

1/4 cup red onion, chopped

1 celery stalk, chopped

1 tablespoon apple cider vinegar

1 teaspoon hot pepper sauce

Salt and black pepper

Instructions:

1. Fill a water bath and set your Joule to 195F/90C.
2. In a large bowl, combine the potatoes, sour cream, mustard, salt, and pepper. Toss well and place in a large zipper lock bag. Remove all air from the bag and submerge in the water bath for 30 minutes.
3. Remove the bag from the water bath and toss the potatoes with the celery, onion, vinegar, and hot sauce. Add more salt and pepper to taste.

Nutritional Info: Calories: 66, Sodium: 54 mg, Dietary Fiber: 1.6 g, Fat: 0.9 g, Carbs: 13.1 g, Protein: 1.8 g.

Beet Salad

Servings: 4 | Prep time: 10 minutes | Cook time: 1 hour

Beets are packed with nutrition and this recipe will show you how to get the best texture and flavor using your Joule sous vide system.

Ingredients:

3 large beets, trimmed and sliced

1/2 cup balsamic vinegar

1 tablespoon olive oil

1/3 cup Parmesan cheese, roughly grated

Salt and black pepper

Instructions:

1. Fill a water bath and set your Joule to 185F/85C.

2. In a large zipper lock bag, combine the beets, vinegar, and a pinch of salt. Remove all air from the bag and submerge in the water bath for 1 hour.

3. Remove the bag from the water bath and toss the beets with the olive oil, salt, and pepper. Top with the Parmesan cheese to serve.

Nutritional Info: Calories: 99, Sodium: 119 mg, Dietary Fiber: 2.5 g, Fat: 4.2 g, Carbs: 12.8 g, Protein: 2.9 g.

Butter Poached Asparagus

Servings: 4 | Prep time: 10 minutes | Cook time: 15 minutes

Asparagus is a perfect companion to meats, fish, as well as poultry. This recipe uses rich butter to pull out those earthy flavors.

Ingredients:

1 pound asparagus, trimmed

4 tablespoons unsalted butter, cut into small pieces

1 teaspoon salt

Instructions:

1. Fill a water bath and set your Joule to 185F/85C.

2. In a large zipper lock bag, arrange the asparagus in a single layer. Evenly distribute the butter pieces throughout the bag and sprinkle on the salt. Remove all air from the bag and submerge in the water bath for 15 minutes.

3. Remove from the water bath and serve. For a little extra kick of heat, add 1/8 teaspoon of cayenne pepper to the bag prior to cooking.

Nutritional Info: Calories: 124, Sodium: 665 mg, Dietary Fiber: 2.4 g, Fat: 11.7 g, Carbs: 4.4 g, Protein: 2.6 g.

7

Poultry

Crispy Chicken Thighs

Servings: 4 | Prep time: 20 minutes | Cook time: 2 hours

The combination of sous vide cooking and pan searing yields the most tender, juicy chicken thighs with perfectly crisp skin.

Ingredients:

4 boneless skin-on chicken thighs

1 clove garlic, peeled and smashed

2 sprigs fresh thyme

2 tablespoons butter

2 tablespoons vegetable oil

Instructions:

1. Fill a water bath and set your Joule to 150F/65C.

2. In a large zipper lock bag, combine place the chicken in a single layer. Add the butter, garlic, and thyme. Remove all air from the bag and submerge in the water bath for 1 1/2 hours.

3. When the chicken is almost finished cooking, get an ice bath ready. Remove the bag with the chicken from the water bath and place directly in the ice bath. Allow to cool for at least 20 minutes.

4. Heat the oil in a large skillet over medium heat. Remove the chicken from the bag and pat dry with paper towels. Season the chicken with salt and pepper and place, skin side down, in the skillet, cooking until the skin is golden brown. Flip the chicken and cook for another 2 minutes. Remove from the skillet and finish with a pinch of kosher salt before serving.

Nutritional Info: Calories: 236, Sodium: 392 mg, Dietary Fiber: 0.5 g, Fat: 18.7 g, Carbs: 1.1 g, Protein: 19.2 g.

Lemon Garlic Chicken

Servings: 4 | Prep time: 10 minutes | Cook time: 45 minutes

This tart and earthy classic is sure to please the whole family, and thanks to your Joule it will always come out tender and juicy.

Ingredients:

4 medium chicken breasts, trimmed and pounded

4 cloves garlic, finely minced

2 tablespoons unsalted butter

2 tablespoons olive oil

Zest and juice from 1 lemon

1/4 teaspoon thyme

1/2 cup white wine

Salt and black pepper

Instructions:

1. Fill a water bath and set your Joule to 145F/63C.
2. Place the chicken breasts, 1 tablespoon of butter, half the garlic, and half of the lemon zest into a large zipper lock bag. Remove all air from the bag and submerge in the water bath for 45 minutes.
3. When the chicken is almost finished cooking, heat a medium saucepan over medium heat. Add the olive oil and remaining garlic and cook for 2 minutes. Then deglaze with the wine and add the thyme and remaining lemon zest. Reduce by half, remove from heat, and stir in the remaining butter and lemon juice.
4. Remove the chicken from the water bath and top with the lemon garlic sauce to serve.

Nutritional Info: Calories: 422, Sodium: 169 mg, Dietary Fiber: 0.5 g, Fat: 23.6 g, Carbs: 3.2 g, Protein: 42.7 g

Sous Vide Fried Chicken Wings

Servings: 10 | Prep time: 15 minutes | Cook time: 3 hours

Believe it or not, your Joule can deliver the juiciest, most tender chicken wings you've ever had.

Ingredients:

10 chicken wings

Salt and pepper for seasoning

1 cup flour

2 cups milk

1 tablespoon salt

2 teaspoons black pepper

1/4 cup cornstarch

2 tablespoons paprika

2 cups vegetable oil

Instructions:

1. Fill a water bath and set your Joule to 154F/68C.

2. Season chicken wings with salt and pepper and place them in a large zipper lock bag. Remove all air from the bag and submerge in the water bath for 3 hours.

3. When the chicken is nearly finished cooking, combine the flour, salt, pepper, paprika, and cornstarch in a large bowl.

4. Heat the oil in a pot to 200F. When the chicken is finished cooking, remove from the bag and pat dry with paper towels. Dip the wings in the milk and then in the dry mixture. Then place the wings in the oil and cook until golden brown. Remove from the oil and allow to cool for several minutes before serving.

Nutritional Info: Calories: 749, Sodium: 847 mg, Dietary Fiber: 0.9 g, Fat: 55.7 g, Carbs: 15.6 g, Protein: 45.4 g.

Chicken Teriyaki

Servings: 2 | Prep time: 30 minutes | Cook time: 2 hours

Did you know that you can use your Joule to make the tastiest chicken teriyaki you've ever had?

Ingredients:

4 boneless skinless chicken thighs

2 tablespoons soy sauce

2 tablespoons brown sugar

2 tablespoons sake

2 tablespoons mirin

2 tablespoons vegetable oil

2 teaspoons fresh ginger, grated

Instructions:

1. Fill a water bath and set your Joule to 149F/65C.
2. In a large zipper lock bag, combine all ingredients, remove air from the bag, and submerge in the water bath for 2 hours.
3. Remove the bag from the water and remove the chicken from the bag. Pour the liquid from the bag into a medium saucepan. Heat until the sauce begins to thicken.
4. Chop the chicken into bite sized pieces and add to the sauce. Serve immediately.

Nutritional Info: Calories: 788, Sodium: 287 mg, Dietary Fiber: 0.4 g, Fat: 35.4 g, Carbs: 19.8 g, Protein: 85.8 g.

Bourbon Chicken Wings

Servings: 6 | Prep time: 5 minutes | Cook time: 2 hours

These sweet and spicy wings have the perfect balance of flavor thanks to a kick of bourbon and pepper that is sure to be a hit at your next party.

Ingredients:

12 chicken wings

1/2 teaspoon salt

1/4 teaspoon black pepper

1/2 cup orange juice

1/2 cup brown sugar

2 tablespoons bourbon

1/2 teaspoon cayenne pepper

2 tablespoons vegetable oil

Instructions:

1. Fill a water bath and set your Joule to 140F/60C.

2. Season the wings with salt and pepper and place them in a large zipper lock bag. Remove all air from the bag and submerge in the water bath for 2 hours.

3. In a medium saucepan, combine the orange juice, brown sugar, and cayenne pepper. Cook until the mixture has thickened slightly. Remove from heat and stir in the bourbon.

4. Remove the wings from the water bath and heat the oil in a medium skillet. Add the wings and cook until browned. In a large bowl, toss the wings with the sauce and serve immediately.

Nutritional Info: Calories: 661, Sodium: 449 mg, Dietary Fiber: 0.1 g, Fat: 26.2 g, Carbs: 14.1 g, Protein: 84.7 g.

Lemongrass Chicken Skewers

Servings: 4 | Prep time: 20 minutes | Cook time: 45 minutes

These light snacks are perfect for entertaining or for a casual family dinner.

Ingredients:

1 pound chicken breast, cut into large chunks

1 stalk lemongrass, finely chopped

2 tablespoons fish sauce

2 tablespoons brown sugar

1 teaspoon salt

1 tablespoon hot pepper sauce

Instructions:

1. Fill a water bath and set your Joule to 150F/65C.

2. In a blender, combine the lemongrass, fish sauce, hot sauce, sugar, and salt, and blend until smooth.

3. In a large bowl, combine the chicken and sauce and stir well. Place chicken on skewers and place in a large zipper lock bag. Submerge the bag and cook for 45 minutes.

4. Remove the bag from the water and place in the refrigerator until cook. Heat a pan over high heat and add the chicken skewers, cooking until seared on all sides.

Nutritional Info: Calories: 63, Sodium: 1296 mg, Dietary Fiber: 0 g, Fat: 1.7 g, Carbs: 5 g, Protein: 6.7 g.

Sous Vide Chicken Stock

Servings: 6 | Prep time: 20 minutes | Cook time: 12 hours

Chicken stock is useful in so many ways, and now you can use your Joule to make the healthiest, most delicious stock you've ever had.

Ingredients:

1 whole chicken carcass

3 cups water

1 stalk celery, chopped

1 carrot, chopped

1 yellow onion, chopped

Instructions:

1. Fill a water bath and set your Joule to 194F/90C.
2. In a large zipper lock bag combine all ingredients. Place in the water bath and cook for 12 hours.
3. Remove the bag from the water and strain. Discard the solids and store the stock in mason jars.

Nutritional Info: Calories: 45, Sodium: 14 mg, Dietary Fiber: 0.7 g, Fat: 2.4 g, Carbs: 2.8 g, Protein: 3.6 g.

Jerk Chicken Thighs

Servings: 2 | Prep time: 10 minutes | Cook time: 2 hours

This Caribbean favorite is easy to make and is sure to come out perfectly every time when you use your Joule sous vide system.

Ingredients:

4 boneless skinless chicken thighs

4 tablespoons olive oil

2 tablespoons hot pepper sauce

1 teaspoon ground cumin

1 teaspoon brown sugar

1 teaspoon ground cinnamon

Salt and black pepper

Instructions:

1. Fill a water bath and set your Joule to 140F/60C.

2. In a large bowl, combine the olive oil, pepper sauce, cumin, sugar, and cinnamon. Season the chicken with salt and pepper and place in a large zipper lock bag. Add the sauce to the bag and submerge in the water bath for 2 hours.

3. When the chicken is almost finished cooking, heat your broiler. Remove the chicken from the bag and arrange on a baking sheet. Broil until slightly charred and serve immediately.

Nutritional Info: Calories: 524, Sodium: 657 mg, Dietary Fiber: 0.7 g, Fat: 36.2 g, Carbs: 14 g, Protein: 38.6 g.

Greek Chicken Meatballs

Servings: 6 | Prep time: 20 minutes | Cook time: 2 hours

These tasty and tender Greek style meatballs are great for as a snack, for entertaining, or even a sandwich.

Ingredients:

1 pound ground chicken

1 tablespoon vegetable oil

1 tablespoon garlic, minced

1 teaspoon fresh oregano, chopped

1/2 teaspoon lemon zest

1/2 teaspoon salt

1/2 teaspoon black pepper

1/4 cup breadcrumbs

Instructions:

1. Fill a water bath and set your Joule to 146F/63C.

2. In a large bowl, combine the chicken, garlic, oregano, lemon zest, salt, pepper, and breadcrumbs. Mix well, and form the mixture into small balls.

3. Place the meatballs in a large zipper lock bag in single layer. Remove all air from the bag and submerge in the water bath for 2 hours. Remove the bag from the water and place in the refrigerator.

4. Heat a skillet with the oil over medium heat. Add the meatballs to the pan and brown each side for several minutes. Remove from the pan and serve.

Nutritional Info: Calories: 185, Sodium: 292 mg, Dietary Fiber: 0.4 g, Fat: 8.2 g, Carbs: 4 g, Protein: 22.6 g.

Sous Vide Penang Curry

Servings: 4 | Prep time: 30 minutes | Cook time: 1 hour

This delightful traditional Thai dish is a little spicy and a little sweet with hints of garlic and chilies for robust flavors everyone will love.

Ingredients:

2 large chicken breasts

1 1/4 cups coconut milk

2 tablespoons vegetable oil

4 tablespoons Penang curry paste

1 tablespoon sugar

1 tablespoon fish sauce

Instructions:

1. Fill water bath and set you Joule to 140F/60C.

2. Place the chicken in a large zipper lock bag. Remove all air from the bag and submerge in the water bath for 1 hour.

3. When the chicken is nearly finished cooking, heat a medium saucepan over medium heat. Add the oil and curry paste and cook until fragrant. Add the coconut milk and cook for 5 minutes.

4. Add the sugar and fish, and continue cooking for another 5 minutes.

5. Remove the chicken from the bag and slice into pieces. Pour the curry sauce over the chicken and serve with steamed rice.

Nutritional Info: Calories: 487, Sodium: 1106 mg, Dietary Fiber: 3.6 g, Fat: 33.1 g, Carbs: 11.3 g, Protein: 36.8 g.

Juicy Sous Vide Turkey Breast

Servings: 6 | Prep time: 10 minutes | Cook time: 3 hours

Tired of dry turkey breast? Well, your Joule is here to save the day with the most tender, juicy turkey you've ever had!

Ingredients:

1 boneless turkey breast

2 tablespoons olive oil

2 tablespoons salt

2 teaspoons black pepper

Instructions:

1. Fill a water bath and set your Joule to 145F/62C.
2. Rub the oil onto both sides of the turkey breast and season with salt and pepper.
3. Place the turkey into a large zipper lock bag, remove all the air from the bag, and submerge the bag in the water bath for 3 hours.
4. When the turkey is nearly finished cooking, heat a cast iron pan to medium-high heat. Remove the turkey from the bag, pat dry with paper towels and sear, skin side down, until golden brown. Rest for several minutes before slicing.

Nutritional Info: Calories: 106, Sodium: 2352 mg, Dietary Fiber: 0.2 g, Fat: 6.6 g, Carbs: 0.5 g, Protein: 11.2 g.

Spicy Turkey Burgers

Servings: 6 | Prep time: 15 minutes | Cook time: 1 hour

These aren't your traditional burgers but because they are so lean and flavorful they may become your favorite burgers.

Ingredients:

2 pounds ground turkey

2 teaspoons salt

1 teaspoon black pepper

2 tablespoons hot pepper sauce

2 teaspoons onion powder

1 teaspoon yellow mustard powder

6 potato buns

6 slices sharp cheddar cheese

Instructions:

1. Fill a water bath and set your Joule to 145F/63C.
2. In a large bowl, combine the turkey, salt, pepper, pepper sauce, onion powder, and mustard. Mix well and form into 6 equal sized patties. Place the patties in two large zipper lock bags, remove all air from the bags, and submerge in the water bath for 1 hour.
3. When the burgers are nearly finished, heat a large skillet over high heat. Remove the burgers from the water bath and sear for one minute per side. Top with cheese, and serve on the buns.

Nutritional Info: Calories: 334, Sodium: 1151 mg, Dietary Fiber: 0.6 g, Fat: 18.6 g, Carbs: 14.2 g, Protein: 29.8 g.

Buffalo Chicken Sandwich

Servings: 4 | Prep time: 10 minutes | Cook time: 1 hour

This zesty take on the traditional chicken sandwich is spicy as well as perfectly tender.

Ingredients:

2 large boneless chicken breasts

1 cup wing sauce such as Frank's Red Hot

Salt and black pepper

1/2 head cabbage, shredded

1/2 cup mayonnaise

3 tablespoons lemon juice

3 tablespoons apple cider vinegar

4 potato buns

Instructions:

1. Fill a water bath and set your Joule to 150F/65C.
2. Season with chicken with salt and pepper and place in a large zipper lock bag. Remove all air from the bag and submerge in the water bath for 1 hour.
3. In a large bowl, combine the mayonnaise, lemon juice, vinegar, and cabbage. Mix well and set aside.
4. Remove the chicken from the water bath, shred, and mix with the wing sauce. Divide the chicken among the buns and top with the cabbage.

Nutritional Info: Calories: 1047, Sodium: 1914 mg, Dietary Fiber: 10.1 g, Fat: 45.5 g, Carbs: 77.2 g, Protein: 86.9 g.

Sous Vide "Smoked" Turkey Leg

Servings: 2 | Prep time: 15 minutes | Cook time: 12 hours

Don't feel like making a whole turkey? Well, you can use your Joule to make perfectly juicy turkey legs any time you want.

Ingredients:

2 turkey legs

1 tablespoon olive oil

1 tablespoon garlic powder

1/2 teaspoon liquid smoke

2 tablespoons curing salt

1 teaspoon black pepper

Instructions:

1. Fill a water bath and set your Joule to 145F/62C.

2. Rub the turkey legs with olive oil and coat with garlic and curing salt. Place in a large zipper lock bag and add the liquid smoke. Remove all air from the bag and submerge in the water bath for 12 hours.

3. When the turkey is nearly finished, heat a large cast iron skillet. Remove the turkey from the bag, pat dry, and add to the skillet, turning frequently until browned on all sides.

Nutritional Info: Calories: 247, Sodium: 72 mg, Dietary Fiber: 0.7 g, Fat: 12.1 g, Carbs: 3.7 g, Protein: 30.1 g.

Duck Breast with Crispy Skin

Servings: 2 | Prep time: 10 minutes | Cook time: 2 hours

Duck breast has a rich earthy flavor that is enhanced by cooking sous vide. The crispy skin adds a delicate crunch that is sure to excite any palate.

Ingredients:

2 skin-on duck breasts

4 tablespoons olive oil

1 tablespoon salt

1 teaspoon black pepper

Instructions:

1. In a large cast iron skillet over high heat, sear the duck, skin side down, for 2 minutes. Remove from pan and allow to cool.

2. Fill a water bath and set your Joule to 135F/57C. Season the duck with salt and pepper and place in a large zipper lock bag. Add the oil to the bag and remove all air. Submerge the bag in the water bath and cook for 2 hours.

3. Remove the bag from the water and heat a cast iron skillet to high heat. Pat the duck dry and sear the skin side once again for 2 minutes. Remove from heat and allow to rest for 5 minutes before slicing.

Nutritional Info: Calories: 401, Sodium: 3531 mg, Dietary Fiber: 0.3 g, Fat: 39.4 g, Carbs: 0.7 g, Protein: 13.2 g.

Duck Leg Confit

Servings: 2 | Prep time: 15 minutes | Cook time: 12 hours

By cooking duck legs for a long period of time with your Joule you will unlock delicious flavors and achieve fall off the bone texture.

Ingredients:

2 large duck legs

2 sprigs thyme

1 tablespoon salt

1 tablespoon pepper

1/2 cup duck fat

Instructions:

1. Rub the duck legs with salt and pepper and place in the refrigerator.
2. Fill a water bath and set your Joule to 170F/76C.
3. Place the duck legs in a large zipper lock bag and add the thyme and duck fat. Remove all air from the bag and submerge in the water bath for 12 hours.
4. When you are ready to serve, heat a large cast iron pan over medium heat and brown the duck legs on both sides.

Nutritional Info: Calories: 149, Sodium: 375 mg, Dietary Fiber: 1.9 g, Fat: 4.8 g, Carbs: 3.8 g, Protein: 22.4 g

8

Pork

Perfect Pork Belly

Servings: 4 | Prep time: 10 minutes | Cook time: 8 hours

Pork belly is so much more than just bacon. This recipe will show you how to braise your belly for silky smooth perfection.

Ingredients:

2 pounds. pork belly

1/2 cup soy sauce

1/4 cup brown sugar

2 cloves garlic, minced

2 tablespoons fish sauce

Instructions

1. Fill a water bath and set your Joule to 170F/76C.

2. In a blender, combine the soy sauce, sugar, garlic, and fish sauce. Blend until smooth.

3. Place the pork belly and marinade in a large zipper lock bag, remove all air from the bag, and submerge in the water bath for 8 hours.

4. When the pork belly is nearly finished cooking, heat your broiler to high. Remove the pork belly from the bag and pat dry with paper towels. Broil for 3 to 4 minutes per side or until slightly charred.

5. Slice thinly to serve.

Nutritional Info: Calories: 130, Sodium: 2499 mg, Dietary Fiber: 0.3 g, Fat: 7.5 g, Carbs: 12.2 g, Protein: 3.9 g

BBQ Pulled Pork Shoulder

Servings: 4 | Prep time: 30 minutes | Cook time: 8 hours

This southern classic comes out tender and flavorful every time when you use your Joule sous vide system.

Ingredients:

1 pound boneless pork shoulder, cut into large chunks

2 tablespoons paprika

2 tablespoons dark brown sugar

2 tablespoons salt

2 tablespoons garlic powder

1 tablespoon ground black pepper

1 tablespoon chili powder

1/2 cup barbecue sauce

Instructions:

1. Fill a water bath and set your Joule to 180F/82C.

2. In a bowl, combine the paprika, sugar, salt, garlic, pepper, and chili powder. Rub the mixture all over the pork and allow to sit for 20 minutes.

3. Place the pork in a large zipper lock bag, remove all air from the bag, and submerge in the water bath for 8 hours. You can leave it in the water bath for up to 12 hours for an even more tender texture.

4. Remove the bag from the water bath and place the pork in a large bowl. Using your fingers or forks, shred the pork and stir in the barbecue sauce.

Nutritional Info: Calories: 260, Sodium: 3926 mg, Dietary Fiber: 3 g, Fat: 7.5 g, Carbs: 22.8 g, Protein: 31.3 g

Sous Vide Pork Tenderloin

Servings: 2 | Prep time: 20 minutes | Cook time: 1 hour

This tender cut is full of flavor but it's also easy to overcook. Thanks to your Joule, you will always have perfectly cooked pork tenderloin.

Ingredients:

1 pork tenderloin

6 sprigs fresh thyme

2 cloves garlic, finely chopped

1 tablespoon olive oil

1 tablespoon butter

Salt and black pepper

Instructions:

1. Fill a water bath and set your Joule to 140F/60C.

2. Season the pork with salt and pepper and place in a large zipper lock bag with the olive oil and thyme. Remove all air from the bag and submerge in the water bath for 1 hour.

3. When the pork is nearly finished cooking, heat a stainless steel or cast-iron pan over high heat until smoking.

4. Remove the pork from the bag, and add the butter to the pan. Place the pork in the pan and use tongs to turn it so that it browns evenly on all sides. Remove from the pan and allow to rest 5 minutes before slicing.

Nutritional Info: Calories: 389, Sodium: 143 mg, Dietary Fiber: 4.8 g, Fat: 19.6 g, Carbs: 9.2 g, Protein: 45 g

Rosemary Pork Chops

Servings: 2 | Prep time: 15 minutes | Cook time: 1 hour

These pork chops are packed with delicious herb flavor and cooked to tender perfection. Never settle for overcooked pork chops again!

Ingredients:

2 bone-in pork chops

1 tablespoon fresh rosemary, chopped

1 tablespoon olive oil

1 tablespoon butter

Salt and black pepper

Instructions:

1. Fill a water bath, and set your Joule to 140F/60C.

2. Season the pork chops with salt and pepper and place in a large zipper lock bag with the olive oil and rosemary. Seal the bag, remove all air, and submerge in the water bath for 1 hour.

3. When the pork chops are nearly finished cooking, heat a cast iron pan over high heat until smoking.

4. Remove the chops from the bag and place in the pan. Add the butter and cook the pork chops for 2 minutes per side, spooning the butter over the chops. Remove from the pan and allow to rest for 5 minutes before serving.

Nutritional Info: Calories: 276, Sodium: 77 mg, Dietary Fiber: 0.7 g, Fat: 25.4 g, Carbs: 1.1 g, Protein: 11.4 g

Sous Vide Pork Shank

Servings: 4 | Prep time: 20 minutes | Cook time: 48 hours

The shank isn't as common as the chop, but if cooked low and slow using your Joule it will be one of the most tender and flavorful cuts of pork you've ever had.

Ingredients:

2 pork shanks

1 can diced tomatoes

1 cup beef broth

3 stalks celery, chopped

2 carrots, chopped

1/2 yellow onion, chopped

1/2 cup red wine

1 tablespoon salt

1 teaspoon black pepper

Instructions:

1.   Fill a water bath and set your Joule to 150F/65C.

2.   In a large zipper lock bag, combine all ingredients and remove all air from the bag.

3.   Submerge the bag in the water bath and cook for 48 hours. Tip: to minimize evaporation in a long cook like this, try covering your cooking vessel in aluminum foil.

4.   Remove the bag from the water and heat your oven to 500F or as hot as it will go. Place the shanks on a baking sheet and cook for 5 minutes to brown.

5.   Pour the remaining contents of the bag into a medium saucepan over medium heat and reduce until slightly thickened.

6.   Remove the shanks from the oven and spoon the sauce over them to serve.

Nutritional Info: Calories: 85.1, Sodium: 115.7 mg, Dietary Fiber: 1.7 g, Fat: 25.4 g, Carbs: 10 g, Protein: 5.1 g

Thai Pork Balls

Servings: 2 | Prep time: 30 minutes | Cook time: 2 hours

These asian-style meatballs are packed with lots of exotic flavors and are cooked to tender perfection thanks to your Joule.

Ingredients:

2 cups ground pork

1 clove garlic, minced

1 tablespoon shallot, minced

2 tablespoon fish sauce

2 small red chilies, de-seeded and finely chopped

2 tablespoons cilantro, finely chopped

1 teaspoon salt

1/2 teaspoon ground white pepper

2 tablespoons fresh lime juice

2 tablespoons vegetable oil

Instructions:

1. Fill a water bath and set your Joule to 150F/60C. In a large bowl, combine all ingredients except the oil, and mix thoroughly.

2. Form the mixture into 12 small meatballs. Place the meatballs into a large zipper lock bag in a single layer. Seal the bag, remove all air from the bag, and submerge in the water bath for 2 hours.

3. When the meatballs are nearly finished, heat a large skillet over high heat. Remove the meatballs from the bag and place in the pan. Cook several minutes per side or until browned. Remove from the pan and serve immediately.

Nutritional Info: Calories: 623, Sodium: 2745 mg, Dietary Fiber: 0.5 g, Fat: 25.4 g, Carbs: 6.4 g, Protein: 88.6 g

Lemongrass Pork Loin

Servings: 4 | Prep time: 15 minutes | Cook time: 2 hours

This pork loin is packed with earthy flavors for a satisfying meal that is easy to make, and is sure to impress the entire family.

Ingredients:

1 pork loin

2 tablespoons coconut oil

1 stalk lemongrass, chopped

1 tablespoon onion, minced

1 tablespoon soy sauce

1 tablespoon brown sugar

2 cloves garlic, minced

2 teaspoons fresh ginger, minced

1 tablespoon fish sauce

1 teaspoon salt

1/2 teaspoon black pepper

Instructions:

1. Fill a water bath and set your Joule to 140F/60C.

2. In a blender, combine the coconut oil, lemongrass, onion, soy sauce, sugar, garlic, ginger, fish sauce, salt and pepper. Blend until smooth.

3. Place the pork loin in a large zipper lock bag and add the marinade. Remove all air from the bag and submerge in the water bath for 2 hours.

4. When the pork is nearly finished cooking, heat a cast iron skillet over high heat.

5.   Remove the pork from the bag and place in the pan, browning on all sides.

Nutritional Info: Calories: 132, Sodium: 1169 mg, Dietary Fiber: 0.3 g, Fat: 9.9 g, Carbs: 4.5 g, Protein: 6.7 g

Sous Vide Carnitas Tacos

Servings: 4 | Prep time: 30 minutes | Cook time: 10 hours

The secret to tender and flavorful carnitas is cooking low and slow. Your Joule adds even more flavor by locking in all those amazing flavors.

Ingredients:

2 pounds pork shoulder, cut into large chunks

1/2 teaspoon ground cumin

1/2 teaspoon oregano

1/2 yellow onion, quartered

1 teaspoon salt

Juice from 1 orange

1 tablespoon lime juice

Corn tortillas

Cilantro to garnish

Instructions:

1. Fill a water bath and set your Joule to 176F/80C.

2. In a large zipper lock bag, combine the pork, cumin, oregano, onion, salt, orange and lime juice. Remove all air from the bag and submerge in the water bath for 10 hours.

3. When the pork is nearly finished cooking heat your broiler. Remove pork from the bag and place on a baking sheet. Broil for 2 to 3 minutes or until browned. Pour the cooking liquid into a blender and blend until smooth.

4. Remove the pork from the broiler and place in a bowl. Shred and add the sauce to taste. Serve with warm corn tortillas.

Nutritional Info: Calories: 694, Sodium: 737 mg, Dietary Fiber: 1.6 g, Fat: 48.7 g, Carbs: 7.9 g, Protein: 53.5 g

Pork Chili Verde

Servings: 8 | Prep time: 30 minutes | Cook time: 24 hours

This green chili is full of subtle flavors and just a hint of heat. Your Joule guarantees that the pork will be perfectly tender.

Ingredients:

2 pounds pork shoulder, cut into chunks

1 tablespoon ground cumin

1 tablespoon olive oil

1 pound tomatillos

2 poblano peppers, seeded and chopped

1/2 onion, finely chopped

4 cloves garlic, chopped

1/2 cup cilantro, chopped

1 cup chicken broth

4 tablespoons lime juice

1 tablespoon salt

1 teaspoon pepper

Instructions:

1. Fill a water bath and set your Joule to 150F/65C.

2. Heat a large cast iron pan with the oil over high heat. Rub the pork with the salt, pepper, and cumin. Sear the pork on all side until browned. Remove from the pan and set aside. Add the tomatillos, peppers, onion, and garlic to the pan, and cook until charred. Remove from the pan.

3. In a blender, combine the vegetables, cilantro, broth, and lime juice. Blend until smooth.

4. In a large zipper lock bag, combine the pork and vegetable puree. Remove all air from the bag and submerge in the water bath for 24 hours.

5. Remove the bag from the water bath and pour contents into a large bowl. Shred the pork, stir well and serve.

Nutritional Info: Calories: 383, Sodium: 1048 mg, Dietary Fiber: 1.6 g, Fat: 27 g, Carbs: 6.4 g, Protein: 28.2 g

Miso Glazed Pork Shoulder

Servings: 8 | Prep time: 45 minutes | Cook time: 24 hours

This dish gets its unique flavor from umami packed miso paste and savory herbs for a pork shoulder that is simply unforgettable.

Ingredients:

4 pounds pork shoulder, cut into chunks

1 tablespoon vegetable oil

1 cup onion, chopped

2 cloves garlic, minced

1 tablespoon fresh ginger, minced

1/2 cup mirin

1/4 cup soy sauce

1/4 cup white miso paste

2 tablespoons brown sugar

Salt and black pepper

Instructions:

1. Fill a water bath and set your Joule to 150F/65C.
2. Heat a large skillet over high heat and add the oil. Sear the pork on all sides and remove from the pan.
3. Turn the heat down to medium and add the onions, cooking until almost browned.
4. Add the garlic and ginger and cook until fragrant. Add the mirin and soy sauce and deglaze. Stir in the miso and sugar and remove from heat.
5. Place the pork and miso mixture in a large zipper lock bag. Remove all air from the bag and submerge in the water bath for 24 hours.

6.   Remove the pork from the bag and set aside. Strain the contents of the bag and pour the liquid into a small saucepan. Cook on medium heat until the sauce thickens.

7.   Combine the pork and sauce and stir well before serving.

Nutritional Info: Calories: 724, Sodium: 735 mg, Dietary Fiber: 0.5 g, Fat: 50.3 g, Carbs: 11.9 g, Protein: 53.6 g

Dry Rub Baby Back Ribs

Servings: 4 | Prep time: 15 minutes | Cook time: 20 hours

These classic ribs taste like they've been cooking in a smoker for days, but your Joule will make sure they are even more tender and juicy.

Ingredients:

2 racks baby back ribs

2 cups barbecue sauce

2 tablespoons paprika

1 tablespoon garlic powder

1 tablespoon onion powder

1 tables chili powder

1 tablespoon salt

2 teaspoons black pepper

2 teaspoons mustard powder

2 tablespoons liquid smoke

Instructions:

1. Fill a water bath and set your Joule to 145F/62C.
2. In a small bowl, combine paprika, garlic, onion, chili, salt, pepper, and mustard. Mix well and rub the mixture all over the ribs.
3. Place ribs in a large zipper lock bag with the liquid smoke. Remove all air from the bag and submerge in the water bath for 20 hours.
4. When the ribs are nearly finished, heat your oven to 450F. Remove the ribs from the bag and arrange on a baking sheet. Cover liberally with the BBQ sauce and cook in the oven for 10 minutes.
5. Remove from the oven, slice into individual ribs and serve.

Nutritional Info: Calories: 1212, Sodium: 3151 mg, Dietary Fiber: 2.9 g, Fat: 83.6 g, Carbs: 51.4 g, Protein: 1.6 g

Pork Milanese

Servings: 2 | Prep time: 30 minutes | Cook time: 50 minutes

This traditional Italian dish is enhanced by your Joule, by locking in extra moisture and flavor.

Ingredients:

2 thin cut boneless pork chops

1/2 cup flour

2 eggs

1/2 cup breadcrumbs

2 tablespoons mustard

2 tablespoons butter

1 clove garlic, chopped

2 sprigs rosemary

2 tablespoons honey

Salt and black pepper

Instructions:

1. Fill a water bath and set your Joule to 155F/68C.

2. Season the pork with salt and pepper and place in a zipper lock bag. Remove all air from the bag and submerge in the water bath for 40 minutes.

3. While to pork cooks, combine the flour, breadcrumbs, salt and pepper in a large bowl. In another bowl, beat the eggs. In a third bowl combine the mustard and honey.

4. Remove the pork from the bag and heat a large skillet over medium heat with the butter.

5. Dip the pork into the eggs and then dredge in the flour mixture. Add the pork to the pan and cook until browned on both sides.

6.   Remove from the pan and serve topped with the mustard sauce.

Nutritional Info: Calories: 668, Sodium: 379 mg, Dietary Fiber: 4.3 g, Fat: 33.5 g,
Carbs: 66.1 g, Protein: 26.7 g

Sous Vide Pork Katsu

Servings: 2 | Prep time: 20 minutes | Cook time: 1 hour

This traditional Japanese fried pork is tender, juicy, and full of complex flavors.

Ingredients:

2 boneless pork chops, pounded

1/2 cup flour

2 tablespoons soy sauce

2 eggs

1 cup panko

2 tablespoons bonito flakes

2 tablespoons salt

2 teaspoons pepper

1/2 cup dashi broth

1 tablespoon vegetable oil

Instructions:

1. Fill a water bath and set your Joule to 135F/57C. Season pork with salt and place in a large zipper lock bag with the soy sauce. Remove all air from bag and submerge in the water bath for 1 hour.

2. In a large bowl, combine the panko, flour, bonito, and pepper. In another bowl beat the eggs and add the dashi.

3. In a large skillet, heat the oil over medium-high heat. Remove the pork from the bags and dip in egg, then dredge in the flour mixture. Place in the skillet and cook until browned on both sides. Remove from pan and serve immediately.

Nutritional Info: Calories: 676, Sodium: 857 mg, Dietary Fiber: 4 g, Fat: 33.5 g, Carbs: 65.9 g, Protein: 33 g

Korean Spare Ribs

Servings: 4 | Prep time: 20 minutes | Cook time: 24 hours

These Korean style ribs are bursting with flavor, and your Joule ensures that the meat is fall off the bone tender.

Ingredients:

2 racks pork ribs

1/4 cup soy sauce

3 tablespoons sugar

1/4 cup green onion, chopped

2 tablespoons garlic, minced

2 tablespoons sesame oil

2 tablespoons toasted sesame seeds

Instructions:

1. Fill a water bath and set your Joule to 145F/62C.

2. In a small saucepan over medium heat, combine the soy sauce, sugar, and garlic. Cook until the sugar has dissolved.

3. Place the ribs in a large zipper lock bag with the soy sauce mixture and sesame oil, and remove all air from the bag. Submerge the bag in the water for 24 hours.

4. Remove the ribs from the bag and set aside. In a small saucepan heat the liquid from the bag and reduce by half. Toss the ribs with the sauce, adding the sesame seeds and green onion before serving.

Nutritional Info: Calories: 244, Sodium: 944 mg, Dietary Fiber: 0.9 g, Fat: 33.5 g, Carbs: 6 g, Protein: 21.8 g

Honey Mustard Pork Chops

Servings: 2 | Prep time: 20 minutes | Cook time: 3 hours

This tangy, sweet take on pork chops is sure to delight your family or guests.

Ingredients:

2 large bone-in pork chops

3 tablespoons olive oil

2 tablespoons whole grain mustard

2 tablespoons honey

Juice from 1/2 lemon

2 tablespoons butter

Salt and black pepper

Instructions:

1. Fill a water bath and set your Joule to 140F/60C.

2. In a bowl, combine the oil, mustard, and honey. Mix well. Place the pork chops in a large zipper lock bag. Add the mustard mixture and remove all air from the bag. Submerge in the water for 3 hours.

3. When the chops are nearly finished, heat a cast iron skillet over high heat. Remove the chops from the bag and sear for 2 to 3 minutes per side and serve immediately.

Nutritional Info: Calories: 996, Sodium: 290 mg, Dietary Fiber: 0.1 g, Fat: 82.7 g, Carbs: 18.5 g, Protein: 45.1 g

9

Beef

Slow Braised Beef Short Ribs

Servings: 4 | Prep time: 20 minutes | Cook time: 24 hours

Cooking these short ribs low and slow using your Joule will result in the most tender fall-off-the-bone short ribs you've ever had.

Ingredients:

2 pounds beef short ribs

1 yellow onion, finely chopped

2 tablespoons vegetable oil

1 cup dark beer

2 sprigs fresh thyme

2 tablespoons tomato paste

3 cloves garlic, minced

Salt and black pepper

Instructions:

1. Fill a water bath and set your Joule to 180F/82C.

2. Season the ribs with salt and pepper. In a dutch oven over high heat, sear the ribs so that they are browned on all sides. Remove and set aside.

3. In a large zipper lock bag, combine all ingredients and remove all air from the bag. Submerge in the water bath for 24 hours.

4. Remove the ribs from the bag and set aside. Pour the liquid from the bag into the dutch oven and reduce by a third. Add the ribs back to the sauce and stir to coat.

Nutritional Info: Calories: 577, Sodium: 149 mg, Dietary Fiber: 1.8 g, Fat: 27.5 g, Carbs: 8.3 g, Protein: 66.8 g

Perfect NY Strip or Ribeye Steak

Servings: 2 | Prep time: 5 minutes | Cook time: 1 hour

This recipe will teach you everything you need to know in order to make perfect medium-rare NY Strip or Ribeye steaks. So simple yet so delicious!

Ingredients:

1 large NY Strip or Ribeye steak

Salt and ground black pepper

1 tablespoon vegetable oil

1 tablespoon butter

Instructions:

1. Fill a water bath and set your Joule to 125F/52C.

2. Season the steak very liberally with salt and pepper on all sides. Tip: For best results allow the steak to rest, salted and peppered, in the refrigerator, uncovered, for at least 4 and up to 24 hours.

3. Place the steak in a zipper lock bag and remove all the air from the bag. Submerge the bag in the water bath for 1 hour.

4. When the steak is nearly finished cooking, heat a cast iron pan over your highest heat to the point that it is heavily smoking.

5. Place the steak in the pan and cook for 1 to 2 minutes, add the butter to the pan, flip the steak and cook another 1 to 2 minutes while spooning the butter over the steak. Remove the steak from the pan and allow to cool for 5 minutes before slicing.

Nutritional Info: Calories: 489, Sodium: 755 mg, Dietary Fiber: 0.7 g, Fat: 25.1 g, Carbs: 1.6 g, Protein: 61 g

Sous Vide Corned Beef

Servings: 12 | Prep time: 20 minutes | Cook time: 48 hours

This traditional Irish favorite isn't just for St. Patrick's Day. Thanks to your Joule, you can make perfect corned beef whenever you want.

Ingredients:

1 (3-5 pounds) beef brisket

1 cup dark beer

1 cup beef broth

2 tablespoons pickling spice

1/2 onion chopped

Instructions:

1. Fill a water bath and set your Joule to 135F/57C.

2. In a large zipper lock bag combine all ingredients, remove all air from the bag, and submerge in the water bath for 48 hours.

3. Remove from the water bath and slice the beef across the grain to serve.

Nutritional Info: Calories: 224, Sodium: 139 mg, Dietary Fiber: 0.2 g, Fat: 7.2 g, Carbs: 1.2 g, Protein: 34.9 g

Beef Tenderloin

Servings: 4 | Prep time: 5 minutes | Cook time: 1 hour

This succulent tenderloin will always come out juicier and more evenly cooked than anything you can make in the oven thanks to the even heat from your Joule.

Ingredients:

2-pound center cut beef tenderloin

2 tablespoons vegetable oil

2 tablespoons butter

Salt and ground black pepper

Instructions:

1. Fill a water bath and set your Joule to 130F/55C.

2. Season the tenderloin very liberally with salt and pepper on all sides. Place in a large zipper lock bag, and remove all air from the bag. Submerge in the water bath and cook for 1 hour.

3. When the beef is nearly finished cooking, heat your oven to 500F or as high as it will go. Remove the beef from the bag and place on a rack over a baking sheet. Cook for 10 minutes or until lightly browned. Remove from oven and allow to cool for 10 minutes before serving.

Nutritional Info: Calories: 578, Sodium: 175 mg, Dietary Fiber: 0 g, Fat: 33.3 g, Carbs: 0 g, Protein: 65.7 g

Slow Cooked Beef Brisket

Servings: 10 | Prep time: 15 minutes | Cook time: 24 hours

Low and slow is the only way to go with tougher cuts like brisket, and your Joule is perfect for maintaining a constant even temperature for perfect results.

Ingredients:

3 to 5 pounds beef brisket

1/3 cup coarsely ground black pepper

1/3 kosher salt

1 tablespoon liquid smoke

2 teaspoons pink salt

Instructions:

1. Fill a water bath and set your Joule to 155F/68C.
2. In a bowl, combine the salt, pink salt, and pepper. Stir well and coat the entire brisket in the mixture.
3. Place the brisket in a large zipper lock bag, remove all air from the bag, and submerge in the water bath for 24 hours.
4. When the brisket is nearly finished cooking, heat a grill or broiler to high heat. Remove the brisket from the bag and pat dry with paper towels. Grill or broil the brisket until a dark crust forms.
5. Remove from heat and allow to cool for 20 minutes. Slice across the grain.

Nutritional Info: Calories: 256, Sodium: 54 mg, Dietary Fiber: 0.3 g, Fat: 8.5 g, Carbs: 0.8 g, Protein: 41.4 g

Sous Vide Beef Back Ribs

Servings: 4 | Prep time: 10 minutes | Cook time: 48 hours

Beef ribs are heartier than pork ribs and your Joule makes sure that they come out just as tender and juicy with a robust flavor.

Ingredients:

1 rack beef back ribs

1/4 cup brown sugar

3 tablespoons paprika

3 tablespoons chili powder

2 tablespoons garlic powder

2 tablespoons onion powder

1 tablespoon fresh thyme, finely chopped

Salt and black pepper

Instructions:

1. Fill a water bath and set your Joule to 146F/63C.
2. In a bowl, combine the sugar, paprika, chili powder, garlic, onion, thyme, salt and pepper. Liberally coat the ribs with the mixture and place in a large zipper lock bag. Tip: If the ribs are too big for one bag, cut the rack into pieces and use more than one bag.
3. Remove all air from the bag and submerge in the water for 48 hours.
4. When the ribs are nearly finished in the water bath, heat your oven to 450F. Remove the ribs from the bag and place on a rack. Bake in the oven for 5 minutes, flip, and bake another 10 minutes.

Nutritional Info: Calories: 281, Sodium: 130 mg, Dietary Fiber: 4.7 g, Fat: 8 g, Carbs: 21.1 g, Protein: 32.9 g

Tender Sous Vide Burgers

Servings: 2 | Prep time: 15 minutes | Cook time: 40 minutes

For the juiciest burgers around try cooking sous vide to lock in flavor. Then finish at high heat for a nice sear.

Ingredients:

1 pound ground beef

Salt and black pepper

Cheddar or American cheese

2 burger buns

Instructions:

1. Fill a water bath and set your Joule to 129F/54C.

2. Form burgers into patties and place them each in its own zipper lock bag. Remove all air from the bags and submerge for 40 minutes.

3. When the burgers are nearly finished cooking, heat a cast iron pan until smoking. Remove the burgers from the bags and place in the pan. Cook for 1 to 2 minutes, flip, top with cheese and cook another 1 to 2 minutes. Remove from pan and serve on the buns.

Nutritional Info: Calories: 448, Sodium: 235 mg, Dietary Fiber: 0.3 g, Fat: 8 g, Carbs: 15.1 g, Protein: 72.3 g

Marinated Beef Kebobs

Servings: 4 | Prep time: 20 minutes | Cook time: 4 hours

This recipe is extremely simple, but packed with amazing flavor and perfect tenderness.

Ingredients:

2 pounds beef chuck, cut into chunks

Salt and black pepper

2 teaspoons rosemary, chipped

1 tablespoon Dijon mustard

1 teaspoon brown sugar

2 tablespoons vegetable oil

Instructions:

1. Fill a water bath and set your Joule to 135F/57C.

2. In a small bowl, combine the salt, pepper, rosemary, mustard, sugar, and oil. Rub the mixture all over the beef chunks and skewer them on bamboo skewers. Place the skewers in a large zipper lock bag. Remove all air from the bag and submerge in the water bath for 4 hours.

3. When the kebobs are nearly finished, light a grill and bring to high heat. Remove the kebobs from the bag and place on the grill for 7 to 10 minutes. Remove and serve immediately.

Nutritional Info: Calories: 489, Sodium: 194 mg, Dietary Fiber: 0.4 g, Fat: 21.2 g, Carbs: 1.3 g, Protein: 69 g

Beef Bourguignon

Servings: 4 | Prep time: 1 hour | Cook time: 16 hours

This traditional French dish full or rich flavors that will be sure to impress your guests for parties or holiday dinners.

Ingredients:

1 1/2 pounds beef chuck roast

4 sliced bacon, thinly sliced

1 tablespoon olive oil

2 teaspoons cornstarch

3 cloves, garlic, minced

2 carrots, chopped

1 onion, chopped

1 bottle red wine

1 cup water

1 cup beef broth

1 tablespoon tomato paste

1 teaspoon thyme

1 bay leaf

4 tablespoons butter

2 tablespoons flour

Instructions:

1. Fill a water bath and set your Joule to 140F/60C.

2. In a large skillet, over medium heat, heat the oil and add the bacon, cooking until browned. remove the bacon from the pan and place inside a large zipper lock bag.

3. Coat the beef in cornstarch, salt and pepper, and sear the beef in the pan used for the bacon. Remove from heat and add the beef to the zipper lock bag.

4. Place the carrots and onion in the skillet and cook until lightly browned then add the garlic and cook for 2 minutes. Add to the zipper lock bag.

5. Add the wine to the pan and deglaze. Then add the water and broth to the pan and simmer or 15 minutes. Add the tomato paste, bay leaf, and rosemary. Pour the wine mixture into the bag and cook for 16 hours.

6. Remove the bag from the water and pour the liquid into a large saucepan over medium heat. Add the flour and butter and stir until the sauce begins to thicken. Add in the rest of the contents of the bag and stir to coat.

Nutritional Info: Calories: 935, Sodium: 854 mg, Dietary Fiber: 2.3 g, Fat: 71.1 g, Carbs: 13 g, Protein: 54.1 g

---

Barbecue Tri Tip

Servings: 4 | Prep time: 10 minutes | Cook time: 6 hours

Grilled tri-tip has excellent flavor, but for an even, pink center, cooking sous vide and finishing over charcoal is the perfect combination.

Ingredients:

2 pounds Tri-tip

1/2 cup barbecue sauce

1 tablespoon brown sugar

Salt and ground black pepper

Instructions:

1. Fill a water bath and set your Joule to 130F/54C.

2. Season the tri-tip with salt and pepper and place in the bag with half of the barbecue sauce. Remove all air from the bag, and submerge in the water bath for 6 hours.

3. Remove the tri-tip from the bag and heat your grill. Dry the tri-tip and mix the brown sugar with the remaining barbecue sauce. Coat the tri-tip with the sauce and grill until browned and caramelized. Slice across the grain to serve.

Nutritional Info: Calories: 457, Sodium: 471 mg, Dietary Fiber: 0.2 g, Fat: 22.2 g, Carbs: 13.5 g, Protein: 46.2 g

Teriyaki Beef and Peppers

Servings: 4 | Prep time: 10 minutes | Cook time: 1 hour

This flavorful beef teriyaki is sure to be a hit with the whole family, and cooking with your Joule guarantees that your beef stays tender and juicy.

Ingredients:

2 pounds flank steak, cut thinly and across the grain

1/2 cup soy sauce

4 tablespoons brown sugar

1 green bell pepper, sliced

1 red bell pepper, sliced

2 tablespoons sesame seeds

2 tablespoons green onion, sliced

2 tablespoons vegetable oil

Instructions:

1. Fill a water bath and set your Joule to 134F/57C.

2. Place the steak, soy sauce, brown sugar, and peppers into a large zipper lock bag. Remove all air from the bag, and submerge in the water bath for 1 hour.

3. When the beef is nearly finished cooking. Heat a large skillet with the oil over high heat. Remove the bag from the water and add all the contents to the pan. Stir for several minutes or until the beef begins to brown. Remove from heat and top with sesame seeds and green onion.

Nutritional Info: Calories: 587, Sodium: 1928 mg, Dietary Fiber: 1.3 g, Fat: 28 g, Carbs: 14.8 g, Protein: 66.3 g

Sous Vide Beef Stew

Servings: 6 | Prep time: 45 minutes | Cook time: 6 hours

This rich and hearty stew can cook all day with no supervision. Just turn on your Joule and get on with your day.

Ingredients:

2 pounds top sirloin, cut into chunks

2 tablespoons butter

1 large russet potato, cubed

1 yellow onion, thinly sliced

2 large carrots, chopped

2 cups red wine

2 cups beef broth

2 pieces bacon, cut into small pieces

2 tablespoons tomato paste

2 cloves garlic, chopped

1 sprig thyme

2 tablespoons flour

Instructions:

1. Fill a water bath and set your Joule to 140F/60C.

2. In a dutch oven, cook the bacon until crispy and remove from the pan. Add the butter to the pan and then add the beef.

3. Brown on all sides and then add the carrots, potatoes, and onion. Add the flour and stir well. Add the tomato paste and cook until fragrant, then add the wine and beef stock. Add the garlic and thyme and remove from heat.

4.   Place mixture in a large zipper lock bag. Remove all air from the bag and submerge in the water bath for 6 hours.
Remove from the water bath and serve.

Nutritional Info: Calories: 428, Sodium: 412 mg, Dietary Fiber: 1.6 g, Fat: 13.9 g, Carbs: 10.3 g, Protein: 48.7 g

---

Hanger Steak with Mushrooms

Servings: 2 | Prep time: 10 minutes | Cook time: 1 hour

Hanger steak is becoming popular because of its delicate texture and robust full flavor. That flavor will be further enhanced by cooking sous vide.

Ingredients:

1 pound hanger steak

1/2-pound crimini or shiitake mushrooms

2 tablespoons vegetable oil

1 clove garlic, minced

1/2 cup dry white wine

2 tablespoons butter

Salt and black pepper

Instructions:

1. Fill a water bath and set your Joule to 130F/54C.

2. Season the steak liberally with salt and pepper and place in a zipper lock bag. Remove all air from the bag and submerge in the water bath for 1 hour.

3. When the steak is nearly finished cooking, heat a cast iron pan to smoking and add the oil. Add the mushrooms and cook until soft.

4. Remove steak from the bag and add to the pan with the mushrooms. Sear on all sides and remove from the pan. Add the garlic and cook until just beginning to brown. Add the wine and simmer until reduced by half. Add the butter, stir well and serve.

Nutritional Info: Calories: 786, Sodium: 459 mg, Dietary Fiber: 2.4 g, Fat: 36.7 g, Carbs: 17.8 g, Protein: 84 g

Filet Mignon with Béarnaise

Servings: 2 | Prep time: 30 minutes | Cook time: 2 hours

This traditional French preparation is made even easier using your Joule to cook sous vide.

Ingredients:

2-8 ounces filets

1/4 cup white wine vinegar

1/4 cup dry white wine

2 tablespoons fresh tarragon, finely chopped

4 egg yolks

6 tablespoons unsalted butter at room temperature

Salt and ground black pepper

Instructions:

1. Fill a water bath and set your Joule to 130F/54C.

2. Season the filets liberally with salt and pepper and place in a large zipper lock bag. Remove all air from the bag and submerge in the water bath for 1 hour.

3. While the filets cook, heat a small saucepan over medium heat. Add the vinegar, wine, and tarragon along with a pinch of salt and pepper. Bring to a boil and simmer until reduced to 1/4 cup. Strain the mixture and let cool.

4. In a bowl, whisk the egg yolks and add the wine mixture once cooled. Mix until smooth. Pour the mixture into a zipper lock bag and remove all the air.

5. When the filets are finished cooking, remove from the water and re-set the temperature on your Joule to 174F/79C. Place the béarnaise in the water bath and cook for 45 minutes.

6.   When the béarnaise is nearly finished, heat a cast iron pan over high heat. Sear the filets for several minutes on each side and remove from heat.

7.   Remove the béarnaise from the water bath, pour into a bowl and whisk until thick and smooth.

Nutritional Info: Calories: 614, Sodium: 643 mg, Dietary Fiber: 0.5 g, Fat: 52.4 g, Carbs: 15.3 g, Protein: 16.6 g

---

Steak Au Poivre

Servings: 2 | Prep time: 15 minutes | Cook time: 1 hour

This old-fashioned steak dish is a staple on steakhouse menus and now you can perfect it at home with your Joule sous vide system.

Ingredients:

2 NY Strip Steaks

1 tablespoon olive oil

3 tablespoons black peppercorns, crushed

4 tablespoons butter

1/2 cup beef broth

1/3 cup brandy

Salt

Instructions:

1. Fill a water bath and set your Joule to 130F/54C.

2. Rub the steaks with oil, salt, and peppercorns. Place the steaks in a large zipper lock bag. Remove all air from the bag and submerge in the water bath for 1 hour.

3. When the steaks are nearly finished cooking, heat a large cast iron skillet over high heat. Remove the steaks from the bag and sear on both sides for several minutes. Remove the steaks from the pan and set aside.

4. Reduce heat to low, add the broth, and boil until reduced by half. Then add the brandy and boil another 3 minutes. Remove from heat and add the butter. Stir until smooth and pour over the steaks to serve.

Nutritional Info: Calories: 874, Sodium: 1125 mg, Dietary Fiber: 025 g, Fat: 70.7 g, Carbs: 7.5 g, Protein: 50.3 g

10

Lamb

Rack of Lamb

Servings: 4 | Prep time: 20 minutes | Cook time: 1 hour

Great for entertaining or anytime, this foolproof rack of lamb is sure to come out perfectly every time.

Ingredients:

2 racks of lamb

1 tablespoon fresh rosemary, chopped

2 cloves garlic, sliced

2 tablespoons vegetable oil

2 tablespoons butter

Salt and ground black pepper

Instructions:

1. Fill a water bath and set your Joule to 130F/54C.

2. Season the racks with salt and pepper, then rub with rosemary. Place the racks into a large zipper lock bag with the garlic. Remove all air from the bag and submerge in the water bath for 1 hour.

3. When the lamb is nearly finished, heat a large cast iron skillet over high heat with the oil. When oil is smoking, add the lamb and brown on both sides. Add the butter to the pan and spoon over the racks. Remove from the pan and serve immediately.

Nutritional Info: Calories: 209, Sodium: 80 mg, Dietary Fiber: 0.4 g, Fat: 16.4 g, Carbs: 1 g, Protein: 14.2 g

Tandoori Lamb Chops

Servings: 2 | Prep time: 15 minutes | Cook time: 3 hours

These exotically flavored chops are sure to be a hit with guests as well as family.

Ingredients:

6 lamb chops

2 tablespoons tandoori paste

2 tablespoon lemon juice

2 tablespoons vegetable oil

2 tablespoons cilantro, chopped

Instructions:

1. Fill a water bath and set your Joule to 140F/60C.

2. Rub the chops with tandoori paste and place in a large zipper lock bag. Remove all air from the bag and submerge in the water bath for 3 hours.

3. When the chops are nearly finished, heat a large cast iron skillet over high heat with the oil. Place the chops in the pan, quickly searing on both sides. Remove from the pan and immediately drizzle with lemon juice. Serve topped with cilantro.

Nutritional Info: Calories: 392, Sodium: 75 mg, Dietary Fiber: 0.1 g, Fat: 21.9 g, Carbs: 6.3 g, Protein: 25.3 g

Lamb Ragu

Servings: 8 | Prep time: 45 minutes | Cook time: 48 hours

This rich and hearty ragu is made even better by cooking low and slow with your Joule, allowing the flavors to fully develop.

Ingredients:

2 lamb shanks

1 can diced tomatoes

1 cup beef stock

1/2 onion, finely chopped

1/2 cup celery, chopped

1/2 cup carrot, chopped

1/2 cup red wine

2 sprigs rosemary

1 tablespoon salt

1 teaspoon ground black pepper

Instructions:

1. Fill a water bath and set your Joule to 150F/65.5C.

2. Combine all ingredients in a large zipper lock bag and mix well. Remove all air from the bag and submerge in the water bath for 48 hours.

3. Remove the bag from the water bath and remove the shanks from the bag. Remove the meat from the shanks and pour the liquid from the bag into a Dutch oven. Heat over medium heat and skim off excess fat. Add the meat to the sauce and stir well before serving.

Nutritional Info: Calories: 90, Sodium: 981 mg, Dietary Fiber: 0.9 g, Fat: 4 g, Carbs: 4 g, Protein: 6.9 g

Lamb Shank Confit

Servings: 4 | Prep time: 20 minutes | Cook time: 48 hours

This decadent dish benefits from cooking for a long period of time to develop serious flavor and delicate texture.

Ingredients:

2 lamb shanks

2 sprigs fresh thyme, finely chopped

1 tablespoon black peppercorns, crushed

1/2 cup duck fat

1 tablespoon salt

Instructions:

1. Fill a water bath and set your Joule to 150F/65.5C.

2. Coat the shanks with salt, pepper, and thyme and place in a large zipper lock bag. Add the duck fat and make sure the shanks are coated. Remove all air from the bag and submerge in the water bath for 48 hours.

3. Remove lamb from the bag and shred before servings.

Nutritional Info: Calories: 314, Sodium: 1870 mg, Dietary Fiber: 1.2 g, Fat: 12.2 g, Carbs: 2.4 g, Protein: 46.3 g

Middle Eastern Lamb Chops

Servings: 2 | Prep time: 10 minutes | Cook time: 2 hours

These exotically flavored chops pair complex spices with lamb's natural richness for a perfectly balanced dish.

Ingredients:

4 lamb loin chops

2 teaspoons Ras El Hanout spice

1 tablespoon olive oil

Salt and ground black pepper

1 tablespoon vegetable oil

Instructions:

1. Fill a water bath and set your Joule to 135F/56.5C.

2. Season the chops with salt and pepper and then coat liberally with the spice blend. Place the chops in a large zipper lock back with the olive oil. Remove all air from the bag and submerge in the water bath for 2 hours.

3. When the chops are nearly finished cooking, heat a cast iron skillet with the vegetable oil over high heat until smoking. Remove the chops from the bag, pat dry with paper towels and sear for several minutes on both sides.

Nutritional Info: Calories: 1339, Sodium: 498 mg, Dietary Fiber: 0.3 g, Fat: 61.8 g, Carbs: 0.7 g, Protein: 183.8 g

Rosemary Leg of Lamb

Servings: 8 | Prep time: 15 minutes | Cook time: 8 hours

A whole leg of lamb is perfect for entertaining, and thanks to your Joule, you can cook and spend time with your guests at the same time.

Ingredients:

2 boneless legs of lamb

2 cloves garlic, finely chopped

2 tablespoons fresh rosemary, chopped

1 tablespoon olive oil

1 tablespoon butter

Salt and ground black pepper

Instructions:

1. Fill a water bath and set your Joule to 130F/55C.

2. Season the lamb with salt and pepper, then in a small bowl, combine the rosemary, garlic, and oil. Rub the rosemary mixture all over the lamb and place in a large zipper lock bag. Remove all air from the bag and submerge in the water bath for 8 hours.

3. When the lamb is nearly finished cooking, heat your broiler to high. Remove lamb from the bag, place on a backing rack and broil for 5 minutes, flip and broil another 5 minutes. While you are broiling, pour the cooking liquid into a small saucepan over medium heat. Reduce by half, and add the butter.

4. Slice the lamb across the grain and serve with the gravy.

Nutritional Info: Calories: 129, Sodium: 131 mg, Dietary Fiber: 0.4 g, Fat: 11.4 g, Carbs: 1.1 g, Protein: 6.1 g

Lamb Vindaloo

Servings: 2 | Prep time: 20 minutes | Cook time: 24 hours

This traditional Indian lamb dish is brimming with amazing flavor and a nice kick of heat.

Ingredients:

1 pound lamb shoulder, cut into chunks

6 tablespoons vindaloo paste

1 tablespoon ghee

1 onion, finely chopped

2 cloves garlic, minced

2 teaspoons fresh ginger, minced

6 tablespoons tomato paste

1 cup water

Instructions:

1. Fill a water bath and set your Joule to 140F/60C.

2. Coat the lamb with the vindaloo paste and place in a zipper lock bag. Remove all air from the bag and place in the water bath for 24 hours.

3. When the lamb is nearly finished, heat the ghee in a Dutch oven and add the onion. Cook until soft, then add the garlic and ginger. Cook until fragrant and add 2 tablespoons of vindaloo paste. Then stir in the water and tomato paste and bring to a boil. Simmer for 30 minutes.

4. Remove the lamb from the bag and add to the sauce. Serve with basmati rice.

Nutritional Info: Calories: 700, Sodium: 1516 mg, Dietary Fiber: 5.7 g, Fat: 36.9 g, Carbs: 28.5 g, Protein: 66.7 g

Dijon Lamb Burgers

Servings: 4 | Prep time: 20 minutes | Cook time: 30 minutes

This fun take on a traditional burger adds the tang of Dijon mustard directly to rich ground lamb for a burger that is truly unforgettable.

Ingredients:

1 pound ground lamb

2 tablespoons Dijon mustard

1/4 cup yellow onion, finely minced

Lettuce

4 tomato slices

4 potatoes or Kaiser rolls

Salt and ground black pepper

Instructions:

1. Fill a water bath and set your Joule to 140F/60C.

2. In a large bowl, combine the lamb, mustard, and onion. Mix well and form into 4 patties. Season with salt and pepper and place in a large zipper lock bag in a single layer. Remove all air from the bag and submerge in the water bath for 30 minutes.

3. When the burgers are nearly finished cooking, heat a large cast iron skillet over high heat. Remove the burgers from the bag and sear for 1 minute per side. Serve on the rolls and top with lettuce and tomato.

Nutritional Info: Calories: 369, Sodium: 189 mg, Dietary Fiber: 5.7 g, Fat: 8.9 g, Carbs: 35.1 g, Protein: 36 g

Lamb Chops with Mint and Apples

Servings: 2 | Prep time: 15 minutes | Cook time: 1 hour

This sweet and savory middle eastern inspired dish has a perfect balance of flavor and texture.

Ingredients:

6 lamb chops

1/4 cup fresh mint, roughly chopped

1 apple, cubed

1 tablespoon lemon juice

1/3 cup Greek yogurt

Salt and ground black pepper

Instructions:

1. Fill a water bath and set your Joule to 140F/60C.

2. Season the lamb with salt and pepper and place in a zipper lock bag. Remove all air from the bag and submerge in the water bath for 1 hour.

3. In another zipper lock bag, combine the mint and apples. Remove all air from the bag and submerge in the water bath.

4. When the lamb is nearly finished cooking heat a large cast iron pan over high heat. Remove the lamb from the bag and sear for 2 minutes per side. Remove the bag with the mint and apples and, in a bowl, combine the mint mixture with the yogurt. Serve the lamb topped with the mint sauce.

Nutritional Info: Calories: 1915, Sodium: 762 mg, Dietary Fiber: 3.5 g, Fat: 72.9 g, Carbs: 17.9 g, Protein: 279.6 g

Herb and Garlic Lamb Kebobs

Servings: 8 | Prep time: 2 hours | Cook time: 1 hour 15 minutes

This savory kebob is perfect for finishing on the grill for a summertime dish that is perfect for backyard cookouts. Salt and pepper to taste.

Ingredients:

2 pounds lamb, cut into chunks

1 cup Greek yogurt

4 cloves garlic, minced

2 tablespoons rosemary

1 teaspoon thyme

2 tablespoons lemon juice

2 green bell peppers, cut into chunks

1 red onion, cut into chunks

Instructions:

1. Fill a water bath and set your Joule to 130F/54C.
2. In a bowl, combine the yogurt, garlic, rosemary, thyme, and lemon juice. Season the lamb with salt and pepper and coat lamb in the yogurt mixture, and skewer.
3. Place skewers in a large zipper lock bag in a single layer. Remove all air from the bag and place in the refrigerator for 1 1/2 hours.
4. Place the lamb skews in the water bath for 1 hour. Skewer the peppers and onions and set aside.
5. When the lamb is nearly finished cooking, light your grill.
6. Remove the lamb from the bags, pat dry with paper towels, and cook on the grill, turning often, for 10 minutes. Add the vegetable skewers to the grill and cook until lightly charred.

Nutritional Info: Calories: 242, Sodium: 93 mg, Dietary Fiber: 1.1 g, Fat: 8.8 g, Carbs: 5.2 g, Protein: 33.7 g

11

Fish

Seared Salmon Filets

Servings: 2 | Prep time: 10 minutes | Cook time: 45 minutes

The secret to perfectly cooked salmon? Sous vide and then sear for perfectly juicy salmon every time.

Ingredients:

2- 6 ounces salmon filets

1 tablespoon olive oil

2 teaspoons salt

Instructions:

1. Fill a water bath and set your Joule to 115F/46C.

2. Rub the salmon with oil and salt, and place in a zipper lock bag. Remove all air from the bag and submerge in the water bath for 45 minutes.

3. When salmon is nearly finished, heat a skillet over medium heat. Remove salmon from the bag and sear, skin side down, for 3 minutes, flip and sear another 2 minutes. Serve immediately.

Nutritional Info: Calories: 610, Sodium: 2950 mg, Dietary Fiber: 2.5 g, Fat: 34.5 g, Carbs: 42.5 g, Protein: 27.5 g

Red Pepper Braised Swordfish

Servings: 2 | Prep time: 20 minutes | Cook time: 45 minutes

This sweet and savory recipe is sure to make your fresh swordfish filets shine with a delightfully light texture.

Ingredients:

1 pound Swordfish filet

1 tablespoon soy sauce

1 tablespoon rice vinegar

1 red bell pepper, cut into thin slices

1 tablespoon fresh ginger, minced

1 clove garlic, minced

1 tablespoon vegetable oil

Instructions:

1. Fill a water bath and set your Joule to 140F/60C.

2. In a large zipper lock bag, combine all ingredients. Remove all air from the bag and submerge in the water bath for 30 minutes.

3. When the fish is nearly finished cooking, heat a skillet with the oil over medium heat. Remove the fish from the bag and sear for 2 minutes per side. Remove from the pan and set aside. Pour the liquid from the bag over the fish to serve.

Nutritional Info: Calories: 435, Sodium: 454 mg, Dietary Fiber: 1.2 g, Fat: 22.9 g, Carbs: 7.5 g, Protein: 48.7 g

Sous Vide Fish Tacos with Mint Salsa

Servings: 4 | Prep time: 30 minutes | Cook time: 30 minutes

These easy fish tacos are sure to come out perfectly tender and the mint salsa is a fresh and lively alternative to traditional salsa.

Ingredients:

1 1/2 pounds cod filets

1 teaspoon chili powder

2 cups fresh pineapple, diced

1/3 cup fresh mint, chopped

2 tablespoons red onion, chopped

2 tablespoons lime juice

1 tablespoon vegetable oil

Flour tortillas

Instructions:

1. Fill a water bath and set your Joule to 135F/57C.
2. Season the fish with chili powder and place into a large zipper lock bag. Remove all air from the bag and place in the water bath for 30 minutes.
3. In a large bowl, combine the pineapple, mint, onion, and lime juice. Mix well and set aside.
4. When the fish is finished cooking, heat the oil in a large skillet. Sear the fish 2 minutes per side and remove from heat. Chop the fish into small pieces and serve with the salsa and tortillas.

Nutritional Info: Calories: 241, Sodium: 128 mg, Dietary Fiber: 2.1 g, Fat: 5 g, Carbs: 14.1 g, Protein: 35.2 g

Salmon Croquettes

Servings: 4 | Prep time: 30 minutes | Cook time: 45 minutes

These delicate salmon cakes make perfect appetizers for entertaining, or make larger ones for a satisfying alternative to crab cakes.

Ingredients:

1 pound skinless salmon filet

2 tablespoons olive oil

2 teaspoons Dijon mustard

2 teaspoons fresh parsley, chopped

2 teaspoons fresh dill, chopped

1/3 cup flour

1 egg, beaten

1/2 cup breadcrumbs

3 tablespoons vegetable oil

Salt and ground black pepper

Instructions:

1. Fill a water bath and set your Joule to 105F/40C.

2. Place salmon and oil in a zipper lock bag, remove all air from bag, and submerge in the water bath for 30 minutes

3. In a bowl, combine the mustard, dill, and parsley, as well as a pinch of salt and pepper. Add the flour, egg, and breadcrumbs, and stir well. When the salmon has finished cooking, shred the filet and add it to the bowl. Form into small balls or larger cakes.

4. Heat a skillet with the oil over medium heat and add the cakes, cooking until browned on both sides.

Nutritional Info: Calories: 512, Sodium: 660 mg, Dietary Fiber: 1.1 g, Fat: 35.1 g, Carbs: 18.2 g, Protein: 32.3 g

Miso Ginger Cod

Servings: 2 | Prep time: 15 minutes | Cook time: 30 minutes

This dish combines sweet and savory for a perfect blend of flavors. Cod is the perfect canvas because of its delicate flavor and texture.

Ingredients:

1 pound cod filets

2 tablespoons white miso paste

1 tablespoon fresh ginger, grated

2 tablespoons soy sauce

2 tablespoons mirin

2 tablespoons brown sugar

2 tablespoons olive oil

2 tablespoons green onion, chopped

Instructions:

1. Fill a water bath and set your Joule to 130F/55C.
2. In a bowl, combine the miso, ginger, soy sauce, mirin, and sugar. Add the fish and coat. Place fish and sauce in a zipper lock bag, remove all air, and submerge in the water bath for 30 minutes.
3. When the fish is nearly finished cooking, heat your broiler. Remove fish from the bag and arrange on a broiling rack. Broil on high for several minutes, or until caramelized. Serve topped with green onion.

Nutritional Info: Calories: 445, Sodium: 1382 mg, Dietary Fiber: 0.6 g, Fat: 16.5 g, Carbs: 21.4 g, Protein: 53.7 g

Lemon Tarragon Salmon

Servings: 4 | Prep time: 10 minutes | Cook time: 45 minutes

Tarragon and lemon pair perfectly with flavorful salmon for a dish that is sure to impress the entire family.

Ingredients:

2 pounds salmon filets

Juice from 1 lemon

1 cup mayonnaise

1 1/2 tablespoons dried tarragon

Salt and ground black pepper

1 tablespoon vegetable oil

Instructions:

1. Fill a water bath and set your Joule to 115F/46C.

2. Season the salmon with salt and pepper. Place in a zipper lock bag, remove all air, and submerge in the water bath for 40 minutes.

3. In a bowl, combine the mayo, lemon juice, and tarragon. When the salmon has nearly finished cooking, heat a skillet with the oil over medium heat. Place the filets in the pan, skin side down, and cook for 2 minutes. Flip and cook another 2 minutes. Remove from pan and top with tarragon sauce to serve.

Nutritional Info: Calories: 467, Sodium: 719 mg, Dietary Fiber: 0.6 g, Fat: 16.5 g, Carbs: 21.4 g, Protein: 53.7 g

Salmon Belly Salad

Servings: 2 | Prep time: 15 minutes | Cook time: 40 minutes

*The belly of the salmon is the fattiest and most juicy part of the fish.
Cooking sous vide ensures that you hang on to all the flavorful juices.*

Ingredients:

1 pound salmon belly

Juice from 2 lemons

Salt and ground pepper

12 ounces arugula

3 tablespoons balsamic vinegar

6 tablespoons olive oil

2 teaspoons Dijon mustard

Instructions:

1. Fill a water bath and set your Joule to 120F/49C.

2. Season the salmon with salt and pepper and place in a zipper lock bag. Remove all air and submerge the bag in the water bath for 30 minutes.

3. When the salmon is nearly finished, combine the oil, vinegar, mustard, and half the lemon juice in a bowl and mix well. Dress the arugula and set aside.

4. Remove the salmon from the bag and cut into small pieces and drizzle with remaining lemon juice. Divide the salad onto plates and top with salmon to serve.

*Nutritional Info: Calories: 191, Sodium: 112 mg, Dietary Fiber: 4.8 g, Fat: 15.5 g,
Carbs: 12.8 g, Protein: 5.5 g*

Sous Vide Ahi Tuna Steaks

Servings: 4 | Prep time: 10 minutes | Cook time: 45 minutes

Rare ahi tuna is always a treat and cooking with your Joule takes all the guesswork out of it.

Ingredients:

2 large tuna steaks

2 tablespoons olive oil

2 tablespoons sesame seeds

Salt and ground pepper

1 tablespoon green onion, chopped

Instructions:

1. Fill a water bath and set your Joule to 105F/41C.

2. Season the tuna with salt and pepper, and place in a zipper lock bag. Remove all air and submerge in the water for 40 minutes.

3. When the tuna is nearly finished, heat a skillet with the oil over high heat. Remove tuna from the bag, pat dry, and sear for 1 minute per side. Remove from heat, cut across the grain and top with sesame seeds and green onions to serve.

Nutritional Info: Calories: 179, Sodium: 34 mg, Dietary Fiber: 0.9 g, Fat: 10 g, Carbs: 2 g, Protein: 20.9 g

Tilapia with Tomatoes and Basil

Servings: 2 | Prep time: 20 minutes | Cook time: 30 minutes

Tilapia is a mild fish that serves as a perfect canvas for robust flavors. And thanks to your Joule it will always come out tender and flaky.

Ingredients:

1 pound tilapia filets

2 tablespoons tomato paste

1 tablespoon olive oil

1 clove garlic, minced

1/2 cup fresh basil, chopped

1/2 cup tomatoes, chopped

2 tablespoons lemon juice

Instructions:

1. Fill a water bath and set your Joule to 134F/57C.
2. In a bowl, combine the oil, tomato paste, garlic, half the basil, tomatoes, and lemon juice.
3. Place the fish in a zipper lock bag and pour in the sauce. Remove all air from the bag and submerge in the water bath for 30 minutes.
4. Remove from the bag and serve topped with the remaining basil.

Nutritional Info: Calories: 382, Sodium: 901 mg, Dietary Fiber: 1.4 g, Fat: 10 g, Carbs: 5.8 g, Protein: 60.2 g

Spicy Garlic Shrimp

Servings: 3 | Prep time: 10 minutes | Cook time: 30 minutes

Everyone loves shrimp and these packs a flavorful kick of heat and are perfectly tender.

Ingredients:

1 pound shrimp, cleaned

1 tablespoon chili flakes

4 cloves garlic, chopped

2 tablespoons mirin or sake

2 teaspoons sugar

2 tablespoons green onion, chopped

Instructions:

1. Fill a water bath and set your Joule to 135F/57C.

2. In a bowl, combine the chili flakes, garlic, mirin, and sugar. Place the shrimp in a zipper lock bag and pour in the chili sauce. Remove all air from the bag and submerge in the water bath for 30 minutes.

3. When the shrimp is nearly finished, heat your broiler to high. Remove shrimp from the bag and place on a baking sheet. Broil for 2 minutes and serve immediately.

Nutritional Info: Calories: 214, Sodium: 457 mg, Dietary Fiber: 0.2 g, Fat: 2.6 g, Carbs: 11.3 g, Protein: 34.8 g

Scallops with Lemon Ginger Broth

Servings: 4 | Prep time: 15 minutes | Cook time: 35 minutes

Scallops need to be cooked just right and thanks to your Joule, you will have scallops that are perfectly tender on the inside with a nice deep sear on the outside.

Ingredients:

1 pound diver scallops

Juice from 2 lemons

1 tablespoon fresh ginger, grated

3 tablespoons butter

1/4 cup white wine

2 tablespoons green onion

Salt and ground black pepper

Instructions:

1. Fill a water bath and set your Joule to 122F/50C.

2. Season scallops with salt and pepper and place in a zipper lock bag in a single layer. Remove all air from the bag and submerge in the water bath for 30 minutes.

3. While the scallops cook, heat a skillet over medium heat and add the wine, ginger and green onions. Cook until reduced by half and pour in a bowl.

4. Remove the scallops from the bag and heat the skillet the high heat. Add the butter to the pan and sear the scallops for 30 seconds per side. Remove from heat and place the scallops in the bowl with the sauce. Stir well and serve immediately.

Nutritional Info: Calories: 170, Sodium: 289 mg, Dietary Fiber: 2.2 g, Fat: 8.8 g, Carbs: 5.4 g, Protein: 14.1 g

Sous Vide Shrimp Cocktail

Servings: 4 | Prep time: 10 minutes | Cook time: 30 minutes

Shrimp cocktail is the perfect appetizer but it can be tricky to cook it just right. Thanks to your Joule, you never have to worry about overcooked shrimp again!

Ingredients:

1 pound large shrimp, cleaned

Cocktail sauce

Lemon wedges

Instructions:

1. Fill a water bath and set your Joule to 135F/57C.

2. Place the shrimp in a large zipper lock bag in a single layer. Remove all air from the bag and submerge in the water bath for 30 minutes.

3. Remove the shrimp from the bag and place directly in an ice water bath. Serve with cocktail sauce and lemon wedges.

Nutritional Info: Calories: 96, Sodium: 177 mg, Dietary Fiber: 0.1 g, Fat: 0 g, Carbs: 3.3 g, Protein: 21.3 g

Spicy Calamari Pasta

Servings: 4 | Prep time: 30 minutes | Cook time: 2 hours

This pasta dish packs lots of fresh flavor and perfectly tender calamari.

Ingredients:

1 pound calamari, cleaned

8 ounces spaghetti

2 tablespoons olive oil

1 teaspoon red pepper flakes

2 cloves garlic, minced

Zest and juice from 1 lemon

Salt and ground black pepper

Instructions:

1. Fill a water bath and set your Joule to 138F/59C.
2. Season the calamari with salt and pepper and place in a zipper lock bag. Remove all air from the bag and place in the water bath for 2 hours.
3. While the calamari cooks, bring a pot of water to a boil and cook the pasta.
4. In a skillet, heat the oil and add the garlic and pepper flakes. Add the spaghetti and turn to coat. Remove the calamari from the bag and add to the pan. Toss well and serve.

Nutritional Info: Calories: 355, Sodium: 72 mg, Dietary Fiber: 0.6 g, Fat: 10.7 g, Carbs: 36.5 g, Protein: 25.9 g

Cod with Lemon Caper Sauce

Servings: 2 | Prep time: 10 minutes | Cook time: 30 minutes

This delicate dish is perfectly flavored with tangy lemon and earthy capers for perfect balance of flavor.

Ingredients:

2 cod filets

1/2 lemon, sliced

1 tablespoon capers

1/4 cup olive oil

Salt and ground black pepper

Instructions:

1. Fill a water bath and set your Joule to 130F/55C.

2. Season cod with salt and pepper and place in a zipper lock bag with a lemon slice on each piece of cod. Add the olive oil and capers. Remove all air from the bag and submerge in the water bath for 30 minutes.

3. Remove from the bag and place on filet on each plate and serve, pouring the sauce over each filet.

Nutritional Info: Calories: 341, Sodium: 203 mg, Dietary Fiber: 0.6 g, Fat: 26.3 g, Carbs: 1.6 g, Protein: 25.3 g

Lobster Rolls

Servings: 2 | Prep time: 15 minutes | Cook time: 30 minutes

This classic New England favorite uses decadent lobster that is cooked to perfection thanks to your Joule.

Ingredients:

2 lobster tails

3 tablespoons mayonnaise

Juice from 1/2 lemon

1 tablespoon butter

Salt and ground pepper

2 soft rolls

Instructions:

1. Fill a water bath and set your Joule to 140F/60C.
2. Bring a pot of water to a boil and cook the tails for 90 seconds. Remove and place in an ice bath. Remove the meat from the shells and place in a zipper lock bag with the butter. Remove all air from the bag and submerge in the water bath for 25 minutes.
3. Remove lobster from the bag and chop into small piece. Place in a bowl and add the mayo, lemon juice, and season with salt and pepper. Serve on the rolls.

Nutritional Info: Calories: 390, Sodium: 1300 mg, Dietary Fiber: 0.7 g, Fat: 19 g, Carbs: 7.3 g, Protein: 48.4 g

Asian Crab Salad

Servings: 2 | Prep time: 20 minutes | Cook time: 1 hour

This decadent crab salad uses traditional Asian flavors to make a perfect salad for a warm summer day.

Ingredients:

2 blue crabs

1/4 cup tomatoes, cubed

1/4 cup cilantro

1 teaspoon chili flakes

2 cups rice noodles

2 cloves garlic, minced

2 tablespoons fish sauce

2 tablespoons lime juice

Instructions:

1. Fill a water bath and set your Joule to 154F/68C.
2. Place the crabs in a zipper lock bag and submerge in the water for 45 minutes.
3. Remove crabs from the bag and remove the crabmeat from the shells. Combine the crab with the garlic, fish sauce, and lime juice.
4. Toss the crab mixture with the noodles, tomatoes, chili flakes, and cilantro, and serve.

Nutritional Info: Calories: 509, Sodium: 315 mg, Dietary Fiber: 2.4 g, Fat: 0 g, Carbs: 50.2 g, Protein: 60.8 g

12

Desserts

Flourless Chocolate Cake

Servings: 6 | Prep time: 30 minutes | Cook time: 1 1/2 hours

This rich cake cooks to perfection using your Joule, and you can keep it warm until you're ready to serve.

Ingredients:

4 eggs

1/2-pound chocolate chips

4 tablespoons butter

Instructions:

1. Fill a water bath and set your Joule to 115F/46C.

2. Place the chocolate and butter in a zipper lock bag and submerge in the water for 15 minutes. Remove and mix until smooth. Reset your Joule to 170F/77. Spray 6 mason jars with cooking spray.

3. Beat the eggs until frothy, and slowly drizzle in the chocolate mixture. Place an equal amount in each jar, seal and submerge in the water for 1 hour. Remove, allow to cool, and serve.

Nutritional Info: Calories: 312, Sodium: 215 mg, Dietary Fiber: 1.3 g, Fat: 21.8 g, Carbs: 22.7 g, Protein: 6.7 g

Sous Vide Cheesecake

Servings: 6 | Prep time: 10 minutes | Cook time: 1 1/2 hours

Everyone loves rich and creamy cheesecake, and your Joule makes the entire process almost effortless.

Ingredients:

12 ounces cream cheese

1/2 cup sugar

1/4 cup crème fraiche

2 eggs

2 teaspoons vanilla

Zest of 1 lemon

Instructions:

1. Fill a water bath and set your Joule to 176F/80C.

2. In a large bowl, combine the cream cheese, sugar, and crème fraiche. Add the eggs one at a time and blend until smooth. Add the vanilla and zest, stir well and pour into 6 mason jars. Seal and submerge in the water for 90 minutes. Remove and allow to cool on a wire rack before serving.

Nutritional Info: Calories: 287, Sodium: 189 mg, Dietary Fiber: 0 g, Fat: 21.4 g, Carbs: 18.5 g, Protein: 6.1 g

Raspberry Ricotta Cake

Servings: 12 | Prep time: 30 minutes | Cook time: 2 hours

This light yet rich cake uses ricotta cheese for a unique texture that is sure to delight your guests.

Ingredients:

12 ounces ricotta cheese

1 cup sugar

8 ounces cream cheese

1/2 cup yogurt

1/2 cup heavy cream

2 tablespoons lemon juice

2 tablespoons flour

1/2 teaspoon salt

1/2 teaspoon vanilla

2 cups graham cracker, crushed

1/2 cup butter

2 cups raspberries

Instructions:

1. Fill a water bath and set your Joule to 170F/77C.
2. In a large bowl, combine the ricotta, 2/3 cups sugar, cream cheese, yogurt, cream, eggs, lemon juice, vanilla, and salt. Remove all air from the bag and submerge in the water for 2 hours.
3. While the filling cooks, combine the graham crackers, butter, and flour in a bowl and mix well. Coat the bottom of a pan with the crust and bake in the oven at 350F for 10 minutes. Remove and cool.

4.   Remove the filling from the water bath and pour into the crust. Place in the refrigerator and cool for 8 hours before topping with the raspberries and serving.

Nutritional Info: Calories: 336, Sodium: 337 mg, Dietary Fiber: 1.8 g, Fat: 20 g, Carbs: 33.8 g, Protein: 6.8 g

Bread Pudding

Servings: 4 | Prep time: 30 minutes | Cook time: 2 hours

This traditional favorite becomes even richer and smoother when cooked in the even heat produced by your Joule.

Ingredients:

1 cup whole milk

1 cup heavy cream

1/2 cup sugar

1/4 cup maple syrup

1 egg and 2 yolks

1 teaspoon vanilla

4 cups brioche bread, cubed

Instructions:

1. Fill a water bath and set your Joule to 170F/77C.
2. In a large bowl, combine all ingredients, mix well, and divide among 4 mason jars. Seal and submerge in the water for 2 hours. Remove the jars and heat your broiler to high. Place jars on a baking sheet and broil until the tops are just browned.

Nutritional Info: Calories: 426, Sodium: 53 mg, Dietary Fiber: 0 g, Fat: 17.4 g, Carbs: 62.3 g, Protein: 6.8 g

Pumpkin Pudding

Servings: 8 | Prep time: 30 minutes | Cook time: 1 1/2 hours

This rich, decadent pudding is perfect for autumn or anytime you're in the mood for the fun flavors of pumpkin spice.

Ingredients:

2 cups canned pumpkin

1 cup brown sugar

1 cup heavy cream

1 cup whole milk

2 teaspoons ground ginger

2 teaspoons ground cinnamon

1 teaspoon ground nutmeg

1/2 teaspoon salt

1/4 teaspoon ground cloves

Instructions:

1. Fill a water bath and set your Joule to 170F/77C.

2. In a large bowl, combine all ingredients and blend until smooth. Pour the mixture into 8 mason jars, seal, and submerge in the water bath for 1 1/2 hours.

3. Remove the jars from the water and cool in the refrigerator before serving.

Nutritional Info: Calories: 164, Sodium: 174 mg, Dietary Fiber: 2.2 g, Fat: 6.9 g, Carbs: 25.5 g, Protein: 2.1 g

Key Lime Pie

Servings: 6 | Prep time: 30 minutes | Cook time: 30 minutes

This tart classic is easy to make and is packed with the unique flavor of delicious Key limes.

Ingredients:

14 ounces condensed milk

1/2 cup key lime juice

6 egg yolks

1 1/2 cups graham crackers, crushed

1/2 cup butter

1 teaspoon salt

3 cups whipped cream

Instructions:

1. Fill a water bath and set your Joule to 180F/82C.

2. In a blender, combine the condensed milk, lime juice, egg yolks, whipped cream, and salt. Blend until frothy. Place in a zipper lock bag and submerge in the water bath for 30 minutes.

3. While the filling cooks, combine the graham cracker, butter, and salt and press into the bottom of a greased pie plate. Bake in the oven at 350F for 10 minutes. Remove from the oven and cool on a wire rack.

4. Remove the filling from the water bath, pour into the crust and refrigerate until cool. The filling will thicken as it cools.

Nutritional Info: Calories: 666, Sodium: 736 mg, Dietary Fiber: 0.8 g, Fat: 46.3 g, Carbs: 55.1 g, Protein: 10.9 g

Classic Chocolate Pudding

Servings: 6 | Prep time: 15 minutes | Cook time: 45 minutes

This classic dessert is so easy to make using your Joule, and it's the perfect end to any meal.

Ingredients:

1 cup whole milk

1 cup heavy cream

1/2 cup powdered sugar

1/3 cup cocoa powder

1/3 cup chocolate chips

3 eggs and 2 extra yolks

Instructions:

1. Fill a water bath and set your Joule to 180F/82C.

2. In a blender, combine all ingredients and blend until smooth. Transfer mixture to a large zipper lock bag and submerge in the water bath for 45 minutes. Mix the contents of the bag halfway through cooking.

3. Remove from the water and pour into a blender. Blend until smooth and place in a bowl. Cool in the refrigerator before serving.

Nutritional Info: Calories: 242, Sodium: 66 mg, Dietary Fiber: 1.7 g, Fat: 15.8 g, Carbs: 20.9 g, Protein: 7 g

Coconut Custard

Servings: 6 | Prep time: 20 minutes | Cook time: 1 1/2 hours

This refreshing custard is made with real coconut for a flavor straight out of the islands.

Ingredients:

4 eggs

1/2 cup sugar

12 ounces coconut milk

2/3 cups whole milk

1/3 cup heavy cream

1/2 teaspoon vanilla

Flaked coconut

Instructions:

1. Fill a water bath and set your Joule to 176F/80C.

2. In a bowl, combine the eggs, sugar, and vanilla. In a medium saucepan over medium heat, combine the coconut milk, milk, and cream.

3. Remove from heat. Gradually add the milk mixture to the egg mixture a small amount at a time. Stir until smooth and pour into 6 mason jars. Seal and submerge in the water bath for 1 hour. Remove from the water bath and allow to cool before topping with the flaked coconut.

Nutritional Info: Calories: 275, Sodium: 63 mg, Dietary Fiber: 1.3 g, Fat: 19.8 g, Carbs: 21.5 g, Protein: 6 g

Cinnamon Spiced Apples

Servings: 4 | Prep time: 20 minutes | Cook time: 2 hours

This delicious spiced apple dessert is great

on its own or paired with a scoop of vanilla ice cream.

Ingredients:

4 green apples, peeled and sliced

2 tablespoons butter

2 tablespoons brown sugar

Juice of 1 lemon

1 tablespoon ground cinnamon

1/4 teaspoon salt

1/4 teaspoon ground nutmeg

1/4 teaspoon vanilla

Instructions:

1. Fill a water bath and set your Joule to 183F/84C.

2. In a bowl, combine the butter, brown sugar, cinnamon, salt, nutmeg, and vanilla. Mix well.

3. In a large zipper lock bag, combine the sauce and apples, and mix well. Remove all air from the bag and submerge in the water bath for 2 hours. Remove from the water and serve while still warm.

Nutritional Info: Calories: 194, Sodium: 192 mg, Dietary Fiber: 6.7 g, Fat: 6.3 g, Carbs: 38 g, Protein: 0.9 g

Do you like FREE cookbooks?

Get a
Free
Cookbook
Every
Month…

Join the
Book
Review
Club
Today!

Healthy Happy Foodie Press

www.JoinTheBookReviewClub.com/R3

95699151R00099

Made in the USA
Middletown, DE
30 October 2018